The Big Picture

As part of Houghton Mifflin's ongoing commitment to the
environment, this text has been printed on recycled paper.

The Big Picture

Idioms as Metaphors

KEVIN KING
Brandeis University

Houghton Mifflin Company   Boston New York

▶ **This book is dedicated to my wife, Ellen Wolff.**

Director of ESL Programs: Susan Maguire
Senior Associate Editor: Kathleen Sands Boehmer
Senior Project Editor: Julie Lane
Production/Design Coordinator: Jennifer Meyer Dare
Senior Manufacturing Coordinator: Sally Culler
Marketing Manager: Patricia Fossi
Marketing Coordinator: Tina Crowley Desprez

Cover Design: Minko Dimov, MinkoImages
Cover Illustration: Mark Steele
Photo credits begin on page 194, which is hereby considered an extension of the copyright page.

Printed in the U.S.A.

Library of Congress Catalog Card Number: 98-72053

ISBN: 0-395-91712-3

9 10 11 12 13 14 15 16 17 18 19 -B- 08 07 06

contents

- Emotional Normalcy Is Togetherness   58

pull yourself together   come apart at the seams
fall apart   crack (me) up
cracked (crackpot)

Unit 5: Money   68

CHAPTER 6

- Money Is Blood   68

make a killing in   to mean business
cut/slash prices   be in the red
cut-throat (competition)   pay through the nose

- Money Is Food   70

dough   reap the benefits/profits
be peanuts (for peanuts)   skim (the) profits

CHAPTER 7

- Money Is Dirty   79

clean (me) out   clean up
take (me) to the cleaners   money laundering
wipe me out   moneygrubber (moneygrubbing)
filthy rich   hit pay dirt
go down the drain/tubes

- Bottom Is Source (of money)   82

foot the bill   have deep pockets
the bottom line

Unit 6: Control   91

CHAPTER 8

- Control Is Contact   91

pin him down   up in the air
get carried away   fly off the handle

- Control Is Hand Contact   93

get a grip   get a hold of yourself
out of my hands   get out of hand
be a soft touch   hit me up for

- Control Is Contact Via Strings   95

pull strings   string me along
at the end of my rope   cut me some slack
rein in   tied to your mother's apron strings

to the student

The Big Picture's approach toward teaching idioms is to treat them as metaphors. To understand this, you need to understand what an idiom is and what a metaphor is.

What Is an Idiom?

An idiom is a word or a group of words whose meaning is not literal. This means that even though you might know the meanings of the individual words in an idiomatic expression, you might misinterpret the meaning of the expression. Idioms are most often used in informal contexts, and the way they are used is determined by convention. For this reason, there are numerous exercises in this text displaying the contexts in which the idiom is usually used.

What Is Metaphor? What Are Basic Metaphors?

A metaphor is a way of understanding one kind of thing in terms of another kind of thing. In other words, you can understand argument in terms of battle, or life in terms of a journey. Compare:

> **a.** The earthquake *destroyed* her house.
>   and
> **b.** They *destroyed* her argument.

In (a) we have the literal meaning of *destroy*. But words cannot destroy other words in the literal sense. So, in (b), *destroy* is used metaphorically. Here, argument is understood in terms of battle.

Similarly, compare:

> **a.** I *walked* into the house.
>   and
> **b.** I *walked* into a new job.

In (a) the meaning of *walked* is literal: it is understood in physical, spatial, non-abstract terms. In (b) *walked* is not physical or spatial. The basic metaphor by which we understand it is that *life is a journey*. These metaphors (**Argument Is Battle** and **Life Is a Journey**) are two of the basic metaphors in terms of which you will learn many idioms. As you will see when doing the warm-up exercises, many of these basic metaphors are common to many languages.

You should realize that not all idioms are metaphors. However, many of the idioms that are hardest to understand can be explained and understood as metaphors. All of the idioms in this text are explained in terms of metaphors, and all are illustrated so that you can see how the idiom and metaphor connect. If you understand *how* an expression means, it is easier to remember *what* it means. And when idioms are changed slightly from their most common form, you will be better able to understand them, because you will know where the idiom comes from metaphorically.

to the teacher

Methodology

Metaphor consists of a source domain and a target domain. In the *Basic Metaphors* of this text, the source domain is the second term and the target domain is the first term. So, in the basic metaphor **Argument Is Battle,** the source domain of "battle" is mapped onto the target domain of "argument." Note that, for the sake of simplicity, the "Are" in basic metaphors like **Ideas Are Balls** is just a shorthand way of saying that ideas are experienced as balls.

We could simply tell students that *bouncing an idea off someone* means to get the person's feedback. But students will have a deeper grasp of the meaning and the idiom will be much more memorable if we inform them that this and numerous other idioms can be explained via the same basic metaphor: **Ideas Are Balls.**

Organization of the Text

The text of 209 idioms consists of eight units, each dealing with a different idiom target domain: Ideas, Knowledge, Argument, Emotion, Money, Control, People, and Life.

Each unit consists of one to two chapters (with the exception of *Life,* which has six chapters). The chapter is the teaching vehicle: Each chapter teaches a group of idioms together under one to five *basic metaphors.*

The unit *Life* has three *derived metaphors.* The idea here is that a basic metaphor sometimes entails other metaphors. For example, if we accept the basic metaphor that **Life Is a Journey,** it quite clearly follows that **Problems Are Barriers to a Journey.**

Each chapter has a brief introductory explanation, followed by a warm-up activity. This activity usually gets students thinking about how metaphor is used in their first languages.

Within each chapter, the organization is consistently as follows:
- Idiom
- Definition
- Picture it!
- Example

The Big Picture provides a commonsense approach to listing the idioms. When the verbs *be* and *get* or other verbs are frequently used with an idiom, these verbs are omitted. Pronouns like *me* or *you* are used in the listing of the idiom in place of *someone.* This helps students to remember the idiom in the way it is used. Hence, you will see **play your cards right** and **level with me.**

Each idiom is illustrated. The section *Picture it!* contains the illustration and a metaphorical explanation of the idiom.

The ample exercises for teaching follow the following format:
- Understanding and Using Idioms
- Conversation Questions
- Understanding and Speaking *or* Understanding, Speaking, and Writing

- Creative Conversation
- Sentence Completion
- Writing and Speaking
- American Art 101
- Rewriting Using Idioms
- Presentation

The exercises build from structured to unstructured, and there is equal emphasis on comprehension and on speaking/active use.

In the *Understanding and Using Idioms* section, have students fill in the blanks with the appropriate idioms. The format for this exercise is almost always a simulated lecture on themes from both science and the humanities. The lectures demand no more specific knowledge than any reading section would demand.

Next is *Conversation Questions.* Have students, in pairs, ask the questions. If possible, the responder should not look at his/her text. Encourage students to give layered answers whenever possible. Invite students to ask you a few of these questions, to show how they can be answered in a realistic way—giving much more than a *yes* or a *no* answer. For example:

Q: My girlfriend (boyfriend) thinks we should get married.
Do you think I should **duck the issue** or confront it?

A: I don't know. Are you in love with her (him)? Are you ready for
marriage? In the United States, people are waiting longer
and longer to get married. I only got married three years
ago, which I guess means that I was **ducking the issue**
for a while. But if you love her (him), go for it.

The great value of these questions consists in their ability to get students talking frankly and learning about one another.

The following exercise, *Understanding and Speaking,* builds on this context, with two students, or a teacher and student, reflecting on and evaluating what has just been said in the lecture (in most cases). This linking device adds an element of authenticity to the text: the reading passage is not an isolated task but part of an academic setting in which the students using this text vicariously participate. The world of students Holden, Bart, Thelma, and Ellen is a metaphor for the world of many students. The context is recycled and evaluated, which helps to reinforce the use and meaning of the idioms.

Providing some variety, the previous exercise alternates with a variant of it called *Understanding, Speaking, and Writing.* Here, students create a conversation by transforming the description of an exchange and replacing italicized definitions of idioms with the idioms themselves.

Creative Conversations are engaging, humorous, and realistic. Students engage in dialogue that is almost antithetical to that of most ESL materials. Taking roles as Harry and Sally or Thelma and Ellen, students engage in realistic situations where they have attitudes. They may, for instance, get angry at each other. Students create the conversation, in part, by varying the structure with fill-ins. Each student listens to his or her partner and replies to the partner's construction of the conversation. Having to remember what a person said is consistent with authentic interchange. In other words, when Harry says, "I work ___(number) hours a day," and Sally has to comment on that, repeating the number, students are allowed to use the idioms in a semistructured way, without just reading a role. And the creativity that is allowed often results in good humor. The teacher can take a role, pairing with a good student, to show how the conversation is done.

Sentence Completion exercises enable students to finish the sentences, thus showing their understanding of the idioms, but within a given context. This is important, since the greatest difficulty with idioms is that the context for using them is intuitive for native speakers, but difficult to teach by description.

Writing and Speaking lets students write their own sentences using the chapter's idioms, but as questions similar to those in the *Conversation Questions* section. Students then ask each other their questions, turning a writing exercise into a speaking exercise. This also allows students to get to know each other better.

American Art 101 is an unstructured writing exercise that follows the academic theme of the book. Have students look at the reproduction of a painting by an American artist and write five sentences about what they see, what is happening, what they feel about the painting, or what one of the people in it might be saying. An example is given in each unit. If you have art books with some of these paintings illustrated in color, bring them in.

Finally, I want to note that register, while very important, is a vast and complex topic that cannot be undertaken in the modest scope of this book. I encourage the individual teacher to help students with this complicated issue.

Acknowledgments

Grateful acknowledgment is made to the following authors and publishers for inspiration in writing this book:

George Lakoff and Mark Johnson, whose work on metaphor provided the pedagogical structure of this presentation of idioms. (See, especially, *Metaphors We Live By*, University of Chicago Press, 1980.)

David Deutsch, Richard Dawkins, Richard Feynman, James Gleick, Jack Cohen and Ian Stewart, Carlos Castaneda, Daniel Dennett, Deborah Tannen, Nelson Goodman, Ray Jackendoff, and Friedrich Nietzsche.

I would like to express my sincere appreciation to the following colleagues for the many valuable suggestions they offered in their review of *The Big Picture*:

Matthew Clements, *California State University—Northridge*
Bob Agajeenian, *University of California at Los Angeles*
Thomas Kozumplik, *Georgetown University*
Marlin Howard, *Indiana University*
Chip DiMarco, *Harvard University*
Martha Hall, *EF Education*
Margo Downey, *Boston University*
Andrea Rico-Elizondro, *El Paso Community College*
Karen Lioy, *University of North Texas*

I also want to express my thanks to Mark Steele for his talent and imagination in creating wonderful illustrations for all of the idioms.

Finally, I want to thank the editorial and production staff at Houghton Mifflin for their support and help in bringing *The Big Picture* to fruition.

K.K.

chapter 1

> **BASIC METAPHORS**
> - Ideas Are Balls
> - Ideas Are Food

INTRODUCTION   In English ideas often are represented as balls or as food. Ideas are communicated from one person to another. In many games we pass balls to one another. Mentally, we use this image of balls being passed to represent ideas being passed from person to person.

Even more common is the representation of ideas as food. Just as food is necessary to keep our bodies going, ideas are necessary to keep our minds going.

The idioms in this chapter deal with simple ideas and also with certain types of ideas (suggestions) or even extensions of ideas (stories). Seeing the idioms as metaphors (in other words, understanding one kind of thing in terms of another kind) makes them easier to understand and to remember.

WARM-UP   How is food used metaphorically in your country? Make a short list of food items and what they represent. For instance, in some countries *cabbage* represents money. In small groups (three or four), share your list of food metaphors. Are there any items that are used similarly in two or more countries? Finally, if you know of any food metaphors in English, tell your group what the food items represent.

IDEAS ARE BALLS

1 **bounce an idea off you**
   Get your opinion

Picture it!
Bounce is what a ball does when you throw it against a wall and it comes back. The *idea* is a ball that I throw against your head and it comes back to me with your impression. In other words, I tell you an idea, and you tell me your impression of it.

Example:
Dr. Chomsky, I have an **idea** I'd like to **bounce off you:** What do you think about the idea that idioms are metaphors?

 toss out a suggestion
Make a suggestion

 catch
Understand, hear

Picture it!
The suggestion is an idea. *Toss* means "throw," and the suggestion is being compared to a ball being tossed.

Picture it!
The idea is a ball. If you *catch* it, you understand it or you have heard it.

Example:
I'd like to **toss out a suggestion:** Coffee should be free for students.

Example:
Did you **catch** what he said? I couldn't hear because the music was too loud.
(**Note:** *You will also hear* **catch on**, *meaning "understand." And you will hear* **catch my drift**, *which means "understand the general direction of my thought."*)

kick around
Discuss, think about

Picture it!
When a group of people give their opinions about an idea, they are kicking that idea (ball) around.

Example:
Bart, I think you should go to Brandeis University, but New York University is also a possibility. Why don't you **kick it around** with your parents and let me know what you think?
(**Note:** *Kick it upstairs means "pass the idea to higher authorities, to your bosses."*)

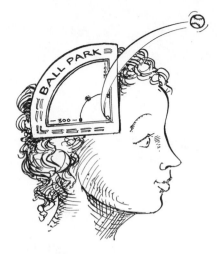

 5 a ballpark figure
A reasonable estimate

Picture it!

The ballpark is a stadium in which baseball is played. An estimate (idea) is a ball that can be hit inside the ballpark or out. The ballpark has definite measurements, so you know approximately how far the ball must go to go out. *Outside* the ballpark is an unreasonable figure; *inside* is reasonable, that is, **a ballpark figure.**

Example:

I asked the mechanic to give me **a ballpark figure** for fixing the radiator in my car, and she said it would be somewhere around $200.

6 field questions
Answer questions

Picture it!

To *field* means to catch bouncing balls on a baseball field.

Example:

Professor Wise is very good at **fielding** tough **questions.**

 7 be on the ball
Be smart, capable

Picture it!

If you are on the ball, you are in close contact with ideas. Therefore, you are smart. Imagine a soccer player who is always close to the ball, or a hitter in baseball who swings his bat and is on the ball.

Example:

If Ralph **were on the ball,** he wouldn't keep missing the bus.
(**Note:** *You will also hear* **have a lot on the ball,** *which means the same as* **be on the ball.**)

 put a spin on it
Provide one interpretation of what someone says

Picture it!

When you throw a ball, you can put a spin on it to make it go right, left, up, or down. What someone says is an idea that can be interpreted in many different ways. Putting a spin on what someone says causes the interpretation to go in the direction you want, just like a ball. You can therefore interpret information the way you want.

Example:

Arnold said that his new movie would be a love story. But when journalists asked him about it later, he **put a** different **spin on it.** He said that people would love the story of the action hero.

IDEAS ARE FOOD

 spill the beans
Reveal a secret

Picture it!

To *spill* is to let something fall out of a container. Of course, you are not supposed to spill beans, and you are not supposed to tell secrets.

Example:

Come on, Sandra, **spill the beans.** Who are you going to the dance with?

leave a bad taste in my mouth
Leave an unpleasant feeling or impression

Picture it!

The idea of an event or a person is experienced as a food that leaves a bad or disgusting taste.

Example:

I had an uncomfortable conversation with my ex-girlfriend about marriage. It **left a bad taste in my mouth.**

 be full of baloney

Have nonsensical ideas (often used to signal disagreement)

Picture it!
Baloney (or bologna) is a kind of sausage. It is widely regarded as bland, that is, having little taste. Thus, baloney represents ideas that are not very good.

Example:
Holden says he is going to get all A's this semester, but I think **that's a lot of baloney.** He never studies. Holden **is full of baloney.**
(**Note:** *You will also hear* **Baloney!** *and* **That's a lot of baloney.**)

 go (be) nuts

Become (be) crazy

Picture it!
A person with nuts in his head instead of ideas will appear crazy.

Example:
Holden wants to ride his bicycle from New York to California! His mother thinks he**'s nuts.**

 be (sound) fishy

Appear dubious or suspicious

Picture it!
If fish has a strong, unpleasant odor, you will suspect that it is not good to eat. Bad ideas are like bad fish.

Example:
I heard that you could get a round-trip ticket from New York to Puerto Rico for just $99, but that **sounds fishy** to me. You probably have to stop in ten cities along the way.

 14 **open a can of worms**

Bring up an idea or subject that makes people uncomfortable; bring up a complex and unexpected problem

Picture it!

Suppose you open a can of food for your guests and it has worms in it. This presents an unexpected problem. You and your guests will feel uncomfortable. Now imagine that this can of food (worms) is the ideas in someone's head.

Example:

When Willy was interviewing for a job as a salesperson, he asked what had happened to the previous salesperson. Willy unknowingly **opened a can of worms** because the interviewer did not want to reveal that the previous salesperson had a nervous breakdown from too much work.

 15 **food for thought**

Interesting idea(s) to think about

Picture it!

Just as food is necessary for the body to develop, ideas are necessary for the mind to develop.

Example:

Ernesto says that large estates should be divided into many small farms and that the land should be redistributed to peasants. That's **food for thought.**

 16 **eat it up**

Believe without question and perhaps foolishly; love it

Picture it!

Just as we can be very attracted to food, we can be very attracted to an idea.

Example:

I didn't do my homework, and I told my teacher that my dog ate it. It wasn't a very good excuse, but the teacher **ate it up!**

 swallow it hook, line, and sinker
Be completely and probably foolishly persuaded

Picture it!
Fish are attracted to lures (artificial fish) with hooks and get caught. The line is the string attached to the fishing pole, and a sinker is a weight that keeps the lure underwater. The fish that swallows the hook, line, and sinker is a foolish fish, because it is going after a false promise of food.

Example:
The used car salesman told us that the two-year-old Mercedes was only $10,000—an amazingly low price—just because the tires were bad, and we **swallowed it hook, line, and sinker.**

 put it on a back burner
Postpone thinking about an issue or working on a project

Picture it!
A stove top usually has four burners, two in front and two in back. The food you are currently working on is usually on a front burner, so you can reach it easily. The food that does not demand immediate attention is put on a back burner.

Example:
Johnny is not going to college for three years, so let's **put that on a back burner** and think about how we're going to pay for this Mercedes today.

Understanding and Using Idioms

Complete the sentences with idioms from the list.

tossed out the idea	*food for thought*	*nuts*
kick around	*on a back burner*	*eat it up*
baloney	*to put my spin on*	
opened a can of worms	*leaves a bad taste in our mouths*	

Food for Thought: Professor Mandel Lectures on Chaos Theory

"You may have heard about chaos theory. Scientists are very excited about it. But what exactly is it? Imagine a butterfly in Beijing stirring its wings, and this results in a hurricane in Costa Rica. Why? Because small changes in initial conditions can have extraordinary effects. Now, before you go thinking that Professor Mandel is completely _____, recall that when Einstein introduced his revolution-

ary concept of relativity, his colleagues didn't all _____. And the theory
                                                            2

really _____ for many moral philosophers, who did not like to see
         3

ethics and morals as relative. But Einstein also pleased many of these moral philosophers

when he _____ that 'God does not play at dice'.* In other words, the uni-
             4

verse did not develop by chance. However, if you will allow me _____ this
                                                                          5

theme, I would say that God *does* play dice, but the dice are unevenly weighted. In

other words, there is some order within the chaos of the universe.

"Putting morality _____ for a while, we will continue our
                               6

look at chaos theory. It may seem a little complicated, but here is another idea for

you to _____ together: why is it that we see trees against a
           7

stormy sky as beautiful, while the sight of a random group of apartment buildings

against any sky _____? The answer is that our feeling of
                         8

beauty is inspired by the harmonious arrangement of order and chaos in natural

objects. The trees represent order and the stormy sky represents chaos. Well, at least

I know that you are listening, because some of you are making faces, as if I were

full of _____. Let me be the first to admit that not everyone
             9

agrees with me. In fact, art critics have always maintained that order is necessary

for beauty, and what I am suggesting is just the opposite! Now there is some

_____."
        10

Continue reading Professor Mandel's lecture, and complete the sentences with idioms
from the list.

spill the beans	*field questions*	*ballpark figure*
on the ball	*fishy*	*catch*
bounce another idea off you	*swallow this hook, line, and sinker*	

"Did you know that our lungs contain more surface area than a tennis court? I

know that sounds completely _____, but it is true. Strange?
                                       11

OK, then let me _____: the length of the coastline of England is
                       12

* dice =

infinite! Look at the coastline from a satellite photograph. Now magnify a part of the photograph and that part of the coastline is longer because there is more detail. Now get closer and it's longer again. And it keeps getting longer the closer and more detailed you get. _____ 13 ?

"I see some of you shaking your heads. Maybe I should stop now and _____ 14 . . . . Nobody? All right, if you don't believe me, tell me how long the coast of England is. Just give me a _____ 15 ."

Bart raises his hand and asks, "Uh, is it, uh, like, four?" The class laughs.

"Now there is a young man who is really _____ 16 . So, young man, if I insisted that the length of the coastline of Japan is infinite, would you _____ 17 ?"

"Gee, I don't know about Japan—I've never been there. But I have been on a tennis court, and I'm pretty sure that my lungs aren't that big. And what about the surface area of the brain? Is that infinite too?"

"Your brain? Well, I think I do know the answer to that, but I won't _____ 18 . "

Conversation Questions

Pair Work. Ask each other the following questions. If your partner asks for additional information, use your imagination to think of something. If you hear a very interesting response, share it with the class.

1. I know you have some plans you haven't told me. Come on, **spill the beans.** What are they?

2. If you could sit down with a small group of Americans who are your age, eat pizza, drink some beer or soda, what subject would you like to **kick around** with them?

3. Have you ever felt hopeless studying some subject and thought that you just couldn't **catch on?**

4. I asked the architect how much it would cost to build a new house. I said, "Give me a **ballpark figure.**" And he said, "$261,394." Why was I so surprised?

5. Let me **bounce an idea off you.** We could go to a baseball game and then have dinner at a French restaurant. Or maybe a Chinese restaurant. What do you think?

6. Do you think your president (or the United States president) is **on the ball?** Why or why not?

7. Is there anyone that you think is **nuts?** What does the person do to make you think so?

8. I'm thinking of telling Professor Mandel that I can't take the final exam this Friday because I have to give the ambassador from my country a tour of the city. Do you think that **sounds** too **fishy?**

9. Would you feel comfortable **fielding questions** about the status of women in your country? Why or why not?

10. Let's **toss out some ideas** about how to improve our English class. Why don't you start the discussion?

11. Would you say that some politician is **full of baloney?** Who and why?

12. Can you think of any action taken by some local or national government that **left a bad taste in your mouth?**

13. Suppose you were having a big party with all your relatives. Could someone **open a can of worms** by mentioning a certain topic or person? What topic, or which person, would that be?

14. Tell me something that you find intellectually interesting. Give me some **food for thought.**

15. There are so many religious cults saying that the world is going to end on a certain day, and lots of people **eat that up.** Why?

16. Some acting teacher told my sister she could be a star in Hollywood, and she **swallowed it hook, line, and sinker.** What should I tell her?

Understanding, Speaking, and Writing

Write a conversation between two students, Thelma and Ellen. For each speech, read the description of what the student wants to say, then transform that information into one or more sentences, replacing each italicized phrase with an idiom. You must write out the entire speech, not just the idiom. Read the conversation with a partner, each partner taking one role. Then switch roles and read the conversation a second time. The first speech is done for you as an example. (Note: To *assent* is to say words like *yeah, yes, OK, hmm, all right,* or *right.*)

Thelma wants to *get Ellen's opinion* on her thoughts about the Scopes trial.

Thelma: *"Could I bounce an idea off you about the Scopes trial?"* or:
    "I want to bounce some ideas off you about the Scopes trial."

Ellen asks if Thelma is referring to the man who was prosecuted by the state of Tennessee for teaching evolution in the 1920s.

Ellen: _____

_____

Thelma assents and adds that people thought that Scopes believed that humans were descended from monkeys, and that *left an unpleasant impression in some people's minds.*

Thelma: _____

_____

It sounds like Scopes was *smart*, but it's too bad he didn't know about DNA. He could have told them that humans differ from pygmy chimpanzees in only about .7% of DNA, but that is just *an approximation.*

Ellen: _____

_____

Thelma is amazed at how close we are, genetically, to chimps. She thinks that is *a very interesting idea.*

Thelma: _____

_____

Ellen thinks that the subject of evolution *was an uncomfortable topic* for thousands of people who believed in a literal interpretation of the Bible.

Ellen: _____

_____

Thelma is glad that she could *discuss* such an interesting issue with Ellen. But if they were discussing it with people who did not believe in evolution, they might have to *put a slightly different interpretation on it.*

Thelma: _____

_____

Creative Conversation

Complete the conversation, using the numbered hints. Read the conversation twice with a partner, changing roles the second time. Do not look at your partner's text. You must remember how your partner filled in the blanks so that you can respond in an appropriate way.

1. animal
2. element or liquid (H_2O, acid, mercury)
3. number
4. person (teaching assistant, husband)
5. threat
6. number ending in zero
7. grade (out of a possible 100; for example, 90, 80, . . .)

Holden: Chaos theory is really fascinating—real **food for thought.**

Bart: It's better than that evolution class we're taking. Personally, I think evolution is **a lot of baloney.** Do you really think we are descended from _____₁?

Holden: (*Joking*) You look like a/an _____.
                                                      1

Bart: But I'm smarter than a/an _____: I've got more **on**
                                                      1
the ball. I changed the data in the chemistry experiment so that it came

out the way it was supposed to. I changed the amount of _____
                                                                    2
from _____ cc to 20 cc. And Professor Mandel **ate**
              3
it up. Still, there is something fascinating about that chaos theory. When

I think about the exam, those butterflies Mandel lectured about start stir-

ring in my stomach—I mean, I get really nervous.

Holden: Well, I'm not worried. I'm going to get an A. I overheard Professor

Mandel talking to her _____ about what's going to
                                            4
be on the exam.

Bart: You did! **Spill the beans,** Holden, or I'll _____.
                                                                    5

Holden: What's it worth to you? Give me **a ballpark figure.**

Bart: About _____ dollars.
                          6

Holden: OK, man, but Professor Mandel is going to think there**'s** something **fishy**

if you get anything higher than _____.
                                                      7

Sentence Completion

Finish these sentences.

1. I'm not sure what to do next year, so let me **bounce an idea off you.** I'm think-

   ing of _____

   _____.

2. My family were talking about politics around the dinner table, and my father

   tossed out an outrageous **suggestion.** He said _____

   _____.

3. My uncle is not really **on the ball.** One night someone came into the house

   downstairs, and my uncle _____

   _____.

4. My father and I were **kicking around** different ideas on how to deal with crime

   and criminals, and I said _____

   _____.

5. I didn't **catch** what Professor Wise just said because _____

_____.

6. Give me **a ballpark figure** for _____

_____.

7. I would feel very comfortable **fielding questions** about _____

_____.

8. The senator had to **put a spin on** his outrageous statement that it was all right

if all the trees in his state were cut down. He said _____

_____.

9. I wish _____ would **spill the beans** about _____

_____.

10. The **fishiest** excuse for missing class I ever heard was _____

_____.

11. The news that **left a bad taste in my mouth** was _____

_____.

12. The newscaster said something that **was** pure **baloney**; she said that

_____

_____.

13. I thought _____ **was nuts** when she _____

_____.

14. My friend really **opened a can of worms** when he asked _____

_____.

15. I think that _____'s idea about _____

is tremendous **food for thought.**

16. The president said that _____

_____, and the people **ate it up.**

17. I told my parents _____

and they **swallowed it hook, line, and sinker.**

18. I _____,

but my girlfriend/boyfriend wants to **put it on a back burner.**

Writing and Speaking

Write six Conversation Questions similar to the ones on pages 9–10, using idioms from this chapter. Then ask and answer these new questions with a partner.

1. _____

   _____

2. _____

   _____

3. _____

   _____

4. _____

   _____

5. _____

   _____

6. _____

   _____

American Art 101

Look at the painting *Christina's World* by Andrew Wyeth (1948) and use five idioms from this chapter to describe what is happening in the painting, or how you feel about the painting, or what the person in the painting might say.

Example: She put all her worries on a back burner and just took a nap.

1. _____

_____

2. _____

_____

3. _____

_____

4. _____

_____

5. _____

_____

Rewriting Using Idioms

Rewrite the following piece of art criticism, using idioms from this chapter and preserving the sense of the passage. You will have to do more than simply substitute phrases for the italicized words: sometimes you will have to change the structure of the sentence.

The paintings of Andrew Wyeth are indeed *interesting and deserving of reflection*. But many serious art critics have never really *understood* what he was doing. One critic said, after looking at an Andrew Wyeth exhibition, that he was relieved to get into a Yellow Cab (taxi) after all the dull brown colors. That critic delighted in *giving his own particular interpretation* of Wyeth's work. But that criticism leaves *an unpleasant impression for other critics*, who love his realism that searches for emotional impact. In "Christina's World," the field and the buildings are dull and relatively colorless. But isn't that part of the feeling that Wyeth wants to capture? Wyeth said of Maine, where this painting was done, that it was like "going to the surface of the moon. I feel things are just hanging on the surface and that it's all going to blow away."

That seems to me perfectly accurate with regard to "Christina's World." If I may *make a suggestion* here—what is vital is what is going on in Christina's mind as she contemplates the things she is looking at. Do you sense loneliness here? Emptiness? Dignity? Had you guessed that Christina, the girl in the painting, had polio?

Though art critics remain unsure about Wyeth's work, the general public *loves it*. And one brave critic said that there was an emotional intensity in the work that was second to none. I, for one, *have been completely persuaded by* that opinion.

Presentation

Prepare a short presentation (up to five minutes) to the class on any topic you wish. Use as many of the idioms in this chapter you feel comfortable with.

> Suggested Topics
>
> The typical day of a student in
>
> _____ (country)
>
> An outstanding scientific discovery
>
> The way language classes should be taught
>
> How to prepare some excellent food

chapter 2

INTRODUCTION It is characteristic of English that intelligence is seen as sharp, and the lack of it as dull. In fact, *sharp* means *intelligent.* We speak of communication as *getting through to someone.* This is consistent with ideas being sharp.

Since we tend to think of intelligence as something that is valuable, it is not surprising that we think of ideas as something that can be bought, sold, or traded—in other words, as commodities.

WARM-UP In your native language, how do you describe a person with good ideas, an intelligent person? Do you use adjectives like *sharp* or *quick*? And how do you describe a person whose ideas are foolish? Translate these descriptions and share them in groups of three or four.

IDEAS ARE SHARP INSTRUMENTS

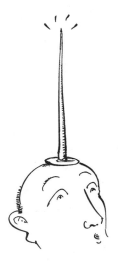

 a point
A focused idea

Picture It!
Because a point is sharp, it can enter easily (into the mind of the listener or reader).

Example:
I see your **point,** professor. If I don't start studying, I will fail the course.

 drive a hard bargain
Negotiate well, without giving up much

Picture It!
To *drive* a nail or a screw is to hit or turn it to make it enter.

Example:
Susan convinced the landlord to reduce her rent by $50 a month. She really **drove a hard bargain.**

 be on the cutting edge
Do the newest and most advanced work or research

Picture It!
A knife has a cutting edge and a dull edge. The cutting edge enters first.

Example:
Our company **is on the cutting edge** of the search for alternative energy sources. We are the first to make a good solar-powered car.

4 **not even scratch the surface**
Deal superficially with an issue or idea
(also: *barely scratch the surface, only scratch the surface*)

Picture It!
To *scratch* is to make a mark on a surface with a cutting instrument. The deeper you go into an issue, the more thoroughly you know it. If your idea does not even scratch the surface of an issue, you do not know the issue very well.

Example:
Isaac wrote a four-page paper on the history of the world. Obviously, he did**n't even scratch the surface.**

5 **be sharp**
Have good ideas, be clever

Picture It!
If your ideas are sharp, you can penetrate the minds of other people.

Example:
Albert Einstein was a **sharp** guy, and so was my uncle Ernie Einstein, who made millions selling bagels and coffee.

6 **hit the nail on the head**
Describe very accurately; comment very astutely

Picture It!
The *head* of a nail is the top. If you hit it on the head (with a hammer), the idea will enter.

Example:
You **hit the nail on the head** when you said this diet would make me thin. I've lost thirty pounds.

IDEAS ARE COMMODITIES

7 a tradeoff
Gaining something while losing something

Picture It!
A commodity is anything that can be bought, sold, or traded. People trade things of nearly equal value, so when you trade, your gain and loss will be nearly equivalent, in theory.

Example:
If I go to France, I will learn a new language, but I will not have as many friends there. I guess it's **a tradeoff.**

8 influence peddling
Receiving money in exchange for using one's influence to get someone to do something

Picture It!
To peddle is to sell. A peddler is a salesperson. Your influence is seen as a commodity that can be bought or sold, like a banana or a pineapple. But influence is the use of one's mental power, or ideas, to change someone's behavior.

Example:
Leon Jones, the brother of President Kenneth Jones, was a well-known **influence peddler.** He **peddled** his **influence** all over the Capitol, taking money from businessmen like Mr. Ross and asking his brother to pass laws to benefit the rich Ross.

9 take into account
Consider an idea

Picture It!
We experience ideas as valuable commodities, just as we experience money as valuable. When you consider an idea, you take it into your mind, just as you put money into your account.

Example:
I'd like to buy a small airplane, but flying is risky, and I must **take** that **into account** in making my decision.

10 **buy that**
Believe an idea

Picture It!

If an idea is a commodity, you can buy it, that is, accept it or believe it. But you don't have to buy the idea, just as you don't have to buy any particular commodity.

Example:

Everyone said the world was flat and if you sailed far enough your ship would go over the edge. But Galileo did not **buy that.** He believed that the world was round.

Understanding and Using Idioms

Complete the sentences with idioms from the list.

cutting-edge	influence peddling	buy
scratched the surface	drive a hard bargain	sharp
hit the nail on the head	take this into account	points
tradeoff		

Professor Paglia Lectures on Gender Differences in Speech

Men and women have a hard time understanding each other because they make

_____ in different ways. Women look for consensus, whereas men
　　　　1

are problem solvers. This difference is evident even in small children, as my

_____ research has shown.
　　　2

Even a seven-year-old boy will _____ in a trade with a seven-
　　　　　　　　　　　　　　　　　3

year-old girl. The boy might get the better of the deal in material terms. He might

even think the girl is not very _____. But their goals are different.
　　　　　　　　　　　　　　　4

The boy needs to feel like a winner, but for the girl, "winning" is just establishing

an agreement. Unfortunately, the boy usually does not _____ when
　　　　　　　　　　　　　　　　　　　　　　　　　5

he judges the transaction.

Now, if you have inferred that this childhood gender difference does not disap-

pear when the boy and girl become husband and wife, you've _____.
　　　　　　　　　　　　　　　　　　　　　　　　　　　　　　　　　6

Who reads the paper every morning—your father or your mother? Your father, in most cases. For him, talk is information. For her, talk is for interaction. It makes you wonder how Mom and Dad get along at all. Conversation, for each one, is a

_____7_____: you can't get just what you expect. As the Rolling Stones sang, "You can't always get what you want."

I don't know if you _____8_____ all this, but observe your parents' conversational habits when you go home. See if I'm telling it as it is.

Oh, my, it's eleven o'clock and we haven't even _____9_____ of this fascinating topic yet. We'll return to it in the next class, when I will attempt to prove that men do more _____10_____ than women, because of their belief that talk is for information, and information, of course, can be sold. That's what *I'm* doing, actually, but in a different way.

Conversation Questions

Pair Work. Ask the following questions. If your partner asks for additional information, use your imagination to think of something. If you hear a very interesting response, share it with the class.

1. Your professor has been explaining something for five minutes, but you still don't see the **point.** What do you do?

2. If you could be **on the cutting edge** of something, what would it be? Why?

3. Are you a person who usually/sometimes/rarely **drives a hard bargain?** What is the last thing you bargained for? Did you drive a hard bargain then?

4. Who is the **sharpest** person you've met in the past year? Why do you think he/she is sharp?

5. If you went to a psychiatrist and she seemed to barely **scratch the surface** of your problem after two sessions, what would you do?

6. My doctor told me that stress was the main cause of people's headaches. Do you think he **hit the nail on the head?**

7. People often say that marriage is a **tradeoff.** What do you think they mean? And do you agree?

8. What kinds of things should I **take into account** before I get married?

9. My uncle always said, "Women—you can't live with them, and you can't live without them." Do you **buy that?**

10. There is a lot of **influence peddling** in Washington. Do you think this is fair? Is it inevitable? What is your view on it?

Understanding, Speaking, and Writing

Write a conversation between two students, Holden and Ellen. For each speech, read the description of what the student wants to say, then transform that information into one or more sentences, replacing each italicized phrase with an idiom. You must write out the entire speech, not just the idiom. Read the conversation with a partner, each partner taking one role. Then switch roles and read the conversation a second time. The first speech is done for you as an example. (Note: To *assent* is to say words like *yeah, yes, OK, hmm, all right,* or *right.*)

Holden asks if Ellen knows who *the Rolling Stones* were.

Holden: *Do you know who the Rolling Stones were?* or:
Do you have any idea who the Rolling Stones were?

Ellen asks if they were jazz players or something. She thought the class was supposed to be about psychology, not ancient history.

Ellen: _____

_____

Holden assents. But Paglia *had better ideas* today than usual. She really *commented very astutely* in the rest of the lecture. Holden's father buries himself in the paper every morning. Holden could come to the breakfast table in a dress and his father wouldn't notice.

Holden: _____

_____

Ellen is not sure if she *believes* that. Her mother reads the newspaper every morning and her father doesn't.

Ellen: _____

_____

Holden asks if it wasn't her father who was fired for *exchanging influence for money.* He thinks he read something about it in the newspaper.

Holden: _____

_____

That was her grandfather, the judge. He was only accused of it, not fired for it. The authorities investigated him, but not thoroughly. They *dealt superficially with the issue.*

Ellen: _____

_____

Holden guesses that for many people real life is *both a gain and a loss:* you lose a little integrity and you get a little money.

Holden: _____

_____

Ellen assents. If her grandfather wasn't *doing the most advanced work in* legal research, she wouldn't be in college. Her family wouldn't be able to afford it.

Ellen: _____

_____

Ellen definitely has *an idea* there. But what about all the stuff they are reading in their ethics course, how making money is not important? Don't they have to *consider that?*

Holden: _____

_____

Ellen's ethics are this: don't cheat your friends. By the way, she will give Holden a ticket to the Indigo Girls concert if he lets her copy his paper on Plato for the ethics course.

Ellen: _____

_____

Holden will do it for a ticket to the concert and anything he wants to drink afterward.

Holden: _____

_____

Ellen assents. Holden *is a tough negotiator.*

Ellen: _____

_____

And Holden wants a summer job at her father's company.

Holden: _____

_____

Now Ellen is *exchanging influence for money!*

Ellen: _____

_____

Holden guesses that it runs in the family.

Holden: _____

_____

Creative Conversation

Complete the conversation, using the numbered hints. Read the conversation twice with a partner, changing roles the second time. Do not look at your partner's text. You must remember how your partner filled in the blanks so that you can respond in an appropriate way.

1. something you read
2. number
3. a subject or topic
4. name of a friend of yours
5. time, later than 10
6. time, later than 10 but earlier than what Sally suggested

Sally: Harry, put down that _____ and talk to me!

1

Harry: What's there to talk about that we haven't already talked about? What's

the **point?** We've been married for _____ years and

2

we've talked about everything under the sun.

Sally: We haven't even **scratched the surface** of anything.

Harry: OK, what do you want to talk about? Choose the subject.

Sally: OK, let's talk about _____.

3

Harry: _____? Oh, I'm **on the cutting edge** of

3

_____. I just have to get my notes on that.

3

Sally: Oh, forget it, Harry. You won't even try. I'm going to

_____'s house.

4

Harry: Whoa! There's no food in the house. Who's going to go shopping?

Sally: Who do you think?

Harry: OK, let's compromise. You stay, and I will not read the

_____ until 10 o'clock.

1

Sally: _____.

5

Harry: _____.

6

Sally: OK. You **drive a hard bargain.**

Harry: You think so? Let's talk about it. . . .

Sentence Completion

Finish these sentences.

1. I didn't understand the **point** you were making about _____

_____.

2. To be **on the cutting edge** of _____,

you have to _____.

3. I think the president of _____

should **drive a hard bargain** on the issue of _____.

4. I think _____ is really **sharp**

because _____

_____.

5. I was talking to my fiancé/friend about _____

but we didn't even **scratch the surface** because _____

_____.

6. _____ **hit the nail on the head** when she said that

_____

is the world's greatest problem.

7. For hundreds of years, we have been dumping _____ into

our rivers. We did not **take into account** that _____

_____.

8. I don't **buy** the argument that _____,

because _____

_____.

9. I could go to New York next week, but I'm not sure I want to. It's really a

tradeoff. I mean, on the one hand, _____

_____,

but on the other, _____

_____.

10. **Influence peddling** occurs because _____

_____.

Writing and Speaking

Write six Conversation Questions similar to the ones on page 22, using idioms from this chapter. Then ask and answer these new questions with a partner.

1. _____
   _____

2. _____
   _____

3. _____
   _____

4. _____
   _____

5. _____
   _____

6. _____
   _____

Presentation

Prepare a short presentation (up to five minutes) to the class on any topic you wish. Use as many of the idioms in this chapter as you feel comfortable with.

Suggested Topics

A holiday in your country

Your opinion of evolution

A painting or an artist you love

Similarities or differences in holiday
   preparations in your country

chapter 3

> **BASIC METAPHORS**
> • Knowledge Is Light
> • Knowledge Is Territory
> • Knowledge Is a Path

INTRODUCTION   The three most common basic metaphors for knowledge are: *knowledge is light, knowledge is a path,* and *knowledge is territory.* These metaphors are shared by many languages. Light enables us to see, and therefore know, but darkness makes seeing and knowing difficult or impossible.

We also conceive of knowledge as territory. We come to know a piece of land by walking across it. As we do, we either create or find a path by which we can explore it and by which we can get to our destination again.

In this chapter, knowledge and understanding are intimately connected. Understanding is the way that we acquire knowledge.

WARM-UP   In your native language, do knowledge and ignorance correspond to light and darkness? If so, can you think of a few expressions that demonstrate the correspondence? Translate them and share them in groups of three or four.

KNOWLEDGE IS LIGHT

 see the light
Come to understand or know

Picture it!
Suppose the sky is covered by dark clouds, so that the day is dark. Then the sun comes out, and everything is bright and clear. Knowledge can come to us like that.

Example:
I struggled as a lawyer for years. Then one day I **saw the light**—I was really meant to be a poet. I was a poet trapped in a lawyer's body.

 see it in a whole new light
Interpret or understand something in a very different way

Picture it!
If knowledge is light, then when a different light shines on something, we know it in a different way. We interpret its meaning differently.

Example:
After I had been working sixty hours a week at the restaurant, I **saw** school **in a whole new light.**

 it dawned on me
Understanding came to me

Picture it!
Dawn is the time of day when the sun comes up. If it dawned on you, then knowledge (light) hit you. The implication that you should have noticed sooner is evident in the fact that dawn appears to all people in the same way. There is irony in the statement that it dawned on *you*. Hey! Wake up! Everyone else sees the light.

Example:
I woke up on my fortieth birthday and **it dawned on me:** I'm not getting any younger. It's time to get married.

 plain as day
Obvious, very clear

Picture it!
The difference between day and night is obvious—day is characterized by light, and therefore is clearly visible.

Example:
Dr. Benway has been working too hard. Look at her eyes. It's as **plain as day** that she needs a vacation.

 beyond the shadow of a doubt
Having certain knowledge

Picture it!
If knowledge is light, then ignorance must be darkness. It follows, then, that doubt must be something in between light and dark—shadows. If doubt is shadow, then moving beyond the shadow is moving into certainty.

Example:
I know **beyond the shadow of a doubt** that Heloise and Mike are in love.

 shed some light on
Clarify, make something known

Picture it!
Shed means *give off* or *throw off*. If knowledge is light, then shedding some light on a thing is making that thing clearer or better understood.

Example:
Inspector Clousseau, the detective, was unable to **shed any light on** the mysterious disappearance of the famous aviator Amelia Earhart.

 be in the dark
Be ignorant or uninformed of something

Picture it!
Knowledge is light, but it is territory as well—a place where you can be. Ignorance, the opposite of knowledge, is seen as the opposite of light.

Example:
We've made some progress in understanding immune-system diseases like AIDS, but we **are still in the dark** concerning a cure.

KNOWLEDGE IS TERRITORY

 cover a lot of ground
Learn a lot of information, teach a lot of material

Picture it!
Cover here means *walk across.* If knowledge is territory, you acquire it by covering it. If a person leads you across that territory, he/she helps you acquire that knowledge.

Example:
We **covered a lot of ground** in English class today. We learned about all the major writers of the seventeenth century.

a blanket statement
A broad generalization, usually not justified in its extent

Picture it!
A blanket covers a lot of ground, or territory, which represents knowledge.

Example:
I heard that commentator on the radio today making **blanket statements** like "All taxes are bad" and "Teenagers today are really lazy."

 as far as I know
In my knowledge (which is incomplete)

Picture it!

If knowledge is territory, and there is a limit to how much a person knows about a particular subject, then that limit can be represented by how *far* in the territory the person is.

Example:

As far as I know, the oil in that can comes from plants that died millions of years ago.

(**Note:** *This is a common idiom that means the same thing is **as far as I can tell**.*)

KNOWLEDGE IS A PATH

 get something across
Make something understood

Picture it!

There is distance between any two people. If I want you to understand something, I must create a path across the distance between you and me.

Example:

Shiko was able to **get his ideas across** this time because his English has improved so much, especially his use of idioms.

along the same lines
In a similar way, displaying similar ideas

Picture it!

Ideas can be written on lines of a page. These lines are a path. Following the same ideas is like following the same lines.

Example:

Reptiles evolved from fish. **Along the same lines,** recent DNA studies have shown that all dogs are descended from wolves.

 beat around the bush
Avoid coming to the point, approach indirectly when speaking

Picture it!
If there is something in the bush that you want, you can go straight to it or keep walking around the bush.

Example:
Romeo, stop **beating around the bush** with all that silly poetry. Do you want to marry me or not?

14 **jump to conclusions**
Make fast and unwarranted conclusions

Picture it!
If knowledge is a path leading to a conclusion, you can jump to the conclusion rather than walk there. That gets you there quickly, but the conclusion will probably not be justified because you have neglected part of the path of knowledge.

Example:
When I met the professional basketball player, I **jumped to the conclusion** that he was American, but in truth he was Canadian.

 come straight to the point
Say what you mean, without digression or unnecessary words

Picture it!
A *point* is an idea. (See Chapter 2.) When you speak, you create a path to understanding that others can follow. The path may be straight, or it may wander.

Example:
Ladies and gentlemen, I know that you are tired, so I will **come straight to the point:** you should elect me president.

 16 on the right track

Correct so far, following the correct line of reasoning

Picture it!

A track is a kind of path. If you are on the right track, you are following the correct line of reasoning.

Example:

The ancient Greeks were **on the right track** thousands of years ago when they said that everything was composed of invisible particles called atoms.

Understanding and Using Idioms

Complete the sentences with idioms from the list.

beyond the shadow of a doubt	*on the right track*	*shed some light*
come straight to the point	*beat around the bush*	*in the dark*
jump to the conclusion	*as far as I know*	*get across*
covered a lot of ground	*blanket statements*	*see the light*
along the same lines	*as plain as day*	*dawned on you*
in a whole new light		

Professor Mann Lectures on Marriage and Marriage Counseling

Today I want to _____ on the subject of marriage. Though I can't
                         1

be certain, _____ the great majority of you are unmarried, but sta-
                      2

tistics tell us that in twenty years, 50 percent of you will have married and

divorced. And the most important thing I can do for you is to explode the myth of

romantic love.

Some of you are surely dismissing me as another old cynic, but I am convinced,

_____, that myths of romantic love are destructive. It is important
            3

that you not remain _____ about these myths or assumptions.
                              4

And what are they? First, we have the myth that people marry because they are

in love. I'll _____: people marry because society expects it. They
                    5

marry out of loneliness, fear for their economic futures, romantic fantasies, and

other neurotic reasons. And _____, we have the myth that romantic
                                        6

love is necessary for a satisfying marriage. Nonsense. Romantic love is selfish,

unnecessary, and often destructive. Because my view is rather extreme, you may be thinking that I have just made a lot of _____ , and I must admit that
7
there are exceptions to my theory.

Now, if you are going to change your perspective and see marriage _____ , we should look at the positive side. What is necessary for a
8
satisfactory marriage? Trust, honesty, clear communication, tolerance, generosity, and respect. Hasn't it _____ that millions of people in the world
9
have arranged marriages and that they divorce a lot less than Americans? Maybe they _____ , and we don't. But don't _____ that I
10   11
am advocating arranged marriages. I'm not.

And if your parents are having a tough time in their marriage, you can suggest that they buy my little book called *Saving Your Marriage*. This will help get them back _____ .
12

One thing I try to _____ in that book is: you have to have good
13
communication skills. For instance, never _____ if you have a com-
14
plaint; instead, say it directly. And avoid negative reciprocity. By that I mean, avoid saying something negative after your spouse says something negative. In other words, don't let the negativity go on like a chain. I hope this is clear for you. For me, it is _____ that negative reciprocity can destroy a marriage.
15

Well, that's enough for today. I think we've _____ . See you on
16
Wednesday, same time, same place. By the way, you can get my book for only ten bucks at the bookstore.

Conversation Questions

Pair Work. Ask each other the following questions. If your partner asks for additional information, use your imagination to think of something. If you hear a very interesting response, share it with the class.

1. With regard to romantic love, do you have foolish ideas, or do you **see the light?** Do you agree or disagree with Professor Mann?

2. Is there anything you **see in a whole new light,** compared to what you thought years ago? How are your ideas different now?

3. Can you think of something which people long ago thought was true **beyond the shadow of a doubt** and which we now know to be false?

4. **It dawned on me** one day that what we call *shooting stars* are not stars at all—they are meteors. Has anything like that ever **dawned on you?** I mean, did you ever have some idea that you later realized was foolish?

5. In my view, it's **as plain as day** that UFOs (unidentified flying objects) exist. Do you agree? Why or why not?

6. Could you **shed some light on** why it's important to learn English?

7. Do you think that adopted children should be kept **in the dark** about their birth parents? Explain.

8. My wife/husband wants to buy a summer house in the Bahamas, and I'm trying to **get across** to her/him that we can't really afford it, but I don't want to destroy her/his dream. What should I say?

9. I'm writing an article about the likes and dislikes of the people in the countries represented by this class. I've mentioned that Indians like spicy food. What can I say, **along the same lines,** about your country?

10. If you were the boss and you had to fire (discharge) an employee, would you **beat around the bush** or come straight to the point?

11. My friend, Muldur, is convinced that aliens from another planet are visiting Earth and that they have unfriendly intentions. Do you think he is **jumping to conclusions?**

12. I'm starting to think that many illnesses are caused by an imbalance in what the Chinese call *qi* (pronounced *chee*), a kind of spirit in us that is hard to explain. Do you think I'm **on the right track?**

13. I'm teaching a course on Asian history this semester. I'm thinking of doing the postwar period, 1947 to the present, in the first week. Do you think I'm **covering too much ground** in one week, or is that the right amount of time?

14. My friend keeps making **blanket statements** about America, like "American food is hot dogs, hamburgers, and pizza." What do you tend to make blanket statements about?

Understanding and Speaking

Pair Work. Complete the conversation with the idioms in the list. Read the conversation with a partner, and then switch roles and read it again.

jump to the conclusion	*it dawned on me*	*see the light*
along the same lines	*in a whole new light*	*in the dark*
beyond the shadow of a doubt		

Bart: Hey, Holden, what did you think of that class today?

Holden: It really depressed me. I'm seeing my relationship with Barbie

_____. I mean, _____ that
                    1   2

maybe we shouldn't be thinking about marriage.

Bart: I guess I'd agree, since you've only known her for a week. It will be hard to tell her, but there's no sense keeping her _____.

3

Holden: Yeah, but don't _____ that I'm irrational because

4
I'm thinking of marriage this soon. I mean, ex-President Nixon proposed marriage to Pat on their first date. He knew _____

5
that he was in love.

Bart: Yeah, and look what happened to him.

Holden: He became president.

Bart: He was the first president who was forced to resign. And

_____, we'll have to resign from Professor Mann's

6
course if we don't buy his book. Can I borrow five dollars?

Holden: I think I'm beginning to _____: buy his book, pass

7
the course.

Creative Conversation

Complete the conversation, using the numbered hints. Read the conversation twice with a partner, changing roles the second time. Do not look at your partner's text. You must remember how your partner filled in the blanks so that you can respond in an appropriate way.

1. amount of money counseling might cost (more than ten dollars)
2. something a man would like to spend money on
3. good, positive reason for interrupting
4. positive reason why your mother should continue living with you
5. something a man would like to do that a woman might not
6. something a woman would like to do that a man might not

Sally: Harry, it's **as plain as day** that we need marriage counseling.

Harry: Why pay some guy with a beard _____ dollars an

1
hour when we can use Mann's book for ten dollars. Hasn't **it dawned**
on you that all the money we save we can spend on

_____?

2

Sally: OK, I'm **in the dark.** What does it say in the book?

Harry: We have to avoid negative reciprocity. In other words, if I say, "Stop interrupting me!" you shouldn't say, "I have to—you talk too much!" That's another negative, see? Instead, you should say something like, "Honey, I'm sorry, but I have to interrupt you because _____."
      Then we're **on the right track.**

Sally: OK. Let's practice. Harry, why does your mother have to live with us?

Harry: Hey, my mother is nicer than yours!

Sally: No! That's negative. You should say, "She has to live with us because _____."
      4

Harry: OK. I **see the light.** We've had our counseling for today. Now let's _____.
      5

Sally: You always want to _____. Why don't we
      5
      _____ instead?
      6

Sentence Completion

Finish these sentences.

1. I used to think that _____, but then I **saw the light:**

   _____.

2. Because _____, I see my relationship with

   _____ **in a whole new light.**

3. I believe, **beyond the shadow of a doubt,** that _____

   _____.

4. One day **it dawned on me** that _____

   _____.

5. It's **as plain as day** that _____

   _____.

6. I wish _____ would **shed some light on** _____

   _____.

7. I don't think that _____ should keep _____

   in the dark about _____.

8. _____ wants to **cover a lot of ground** when we meet to

   _____.

9. _____ made **a blanket statement** about _____.

   She said _____.

10. **As far as I know,** _____.

11. The reason why I failed to **get across** my idea that _____

   is that _____.

12. In general, to make a marriage work, men need to _____,

   and **along the same lines,** _____.

13. I could ramble for an hour about _____, but I'll **come**

   straight to the point: _____.

14. _____ just **beat around the bush** when I asked her

   _____, because _____.

15. Don't go **jumping to conclusions!** Just because you saw me

   _____, that doesn't mean that _____.

16. President _____ would be **on the right track** if he

   _____.

Writing and Speaking

Write six Conversation Questions similar to the ones on pages 34–35, using idioms from this chapter. Then ask and answer these new questions with a partner.

1. _____

   _____

2. _____

   _____

3. _____

   _____

4. _____

   _____

5. _____

_____

6. _____

_____

American Art 101

Look at the painting *#49 The Migration Series* ("They also found discrimination in the North") by Jacob Lawrence and use five idioms from this chapter to tell what is happening in the painting, or how you feel about the painting, or what one of the people in the painting might say.

Example: Lawrence seems to come straight to the point—racial discrimination was very strong.

1. _____

_____

2. _____

_____

3. _____

_____

4. _____

_____

5. _____

_____

Rewriting Using Idioms

Rewrite the following piece of art criticism, using idioms from this chapter and preserving the sense of the passage. You will have to do more than simply substitute phrases: sometimes you will have to change the structure of the sentence.

Jacob Lawrence's "Migration Series" is a stunning depiction of the history of race relations in the United States. Lawrence *clarifies* the problems that blacks encountered in the nineteenth century when migrating from the South to the North after the Civil War. Anyone who thought that freedom from slavery guaranteed equal treatment quickly *understood:* discrimination was everywhere. *Broad generalizations* like "We are free at last" were revealed to be only half-truths.

Lawrence *makes this understood* by showing tables marked "Blacks only." It was *very clear* that prejudice would not disappear overnight.

Presentation

Prepare a short presentation (up to five minutes) to the class on any topic you wish. Use as many of the idioms in this chapter as you feel comfortable with.

> Suggested Topics
>
> Arranged marriages
>
> How to drive your spouse crazy
>
> What qualities to look for in a potential
>   spouse
>
> The biggest problem in marriage
>
> Some blanket statement that is false
>
> What I see in a whole new light

chapter 4

BASIC METAPHORS
- An Argument Is a Vehicle
- An Argument Is a Construction
- An Argument Is a Battle

INTRODUCTION If *life is a journey* and *knowledge is a path*, then an argument is a vehicle that moves along that path on that journey. *Argument* here means "a coherent series of reasons"; it is similar to a discussion. Think of what a vehicle does: it transports people or things from a starting point to a destination. Now look at an argument in the same way: by means of your argument you transport your ideas from your mind to other minds.

Just as we construct a building, we construct an argument. The process is very similar. An argument proceeds step by step, adding idea to idea, and a building is made in the same way, adding stones, bricks, and other materials.

And just as we fight in battle, we fight in an argument. In ordinary language, we use this metaphor often.

Note: *Many of the idioms in this chapter are used to structure lectures and presentations. Students (especially international teaching assistants) who may need to give lectures or presentations should learn these well.*

WARM-UP Think of the things you would do if you were driving a car or a train. In your native language, can any of these expressions be used in making an argument? Now think of constructing a building. Are there any steps that could apply to constructing an argument? Finally, think about fighting in a battle. Can any of the things you do be applied to having a verbal argument? Share your answers in groups of three or four.

AN ARGUMENT IS A VEHICLE

 1 jump in
Enter a discussion, interrupt

Picture it!
To jump in a car is to get in quickly.

Example:
Student: Can I **jump in?** I want to **jump in.**
Teacher: Sure.
Student: OK, I think metaphors are a good way to explain idioms.

 get sidetracked
Digress, deal with something unrelated to the main point

Picture it!
The argument here is a train. It has a main track, which corresponds to the main point of an argument. There are side tracks that don't lead to the main destination.

Example:
Professor Wise: Sorry I **got sidetracked** there for a moment—I thought you'd be interested to know that the president and I both dated the same girl in high school. Anyway, let's get back to our discussion of education in California.

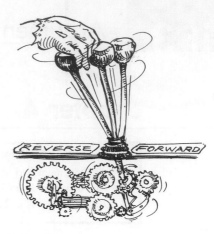

 switch gears
Go to another topic

Picture it!
A car's transmission may have three, four, or five gears. With a standard transmission you change gears, and in your argument you change topics.

Example:
All right, we've been discussing global politics. Now I want to **switch gears** and talk about global economics.
(**Note:** *You will also hear* ***change gears.***)

 (Let me) put it this way
Express it in a way that fits my audience

Picture it!
The argument is a vehicle that can take different roads or tracks. For some people it is better to go one way, and for other people another way.

Example:
Galileo was a great scientist. **Let me put it this way:** if Galileo had never lived, science would not have progressed so rapidly.

 5 **jump on the bandwagon**
Follow the popular movement, say what everybody is saying, do what everybody is doing

Picture it!
In nineteenth-century elections there was often a band riding on the back of a wagon to draw the attention of voters. Those who liked the candidate or his music jumped on the bandwagon.

Example:
Everyone wants lower taxes these days. The governor will have to **jump on the bandwagon** or she will lose the next election.

AN ARGUMENT IS A CONSTRUCTION

 6 **be on shaky ground**
Have an argument with a weak basis

Picture it!
If there is an earthquake, the ground shakes. A good argument should be on firm ground.

Example:
You are **on shaky ground** when you say that all American food is bad. I had a delicious hamburger last night, with raw onion and tomatoes on it.

7 **can't get a word in edgewise**
Find it impossible to speak because another person will not stop talking

Picture it!
Because the edge is sharp, it can be inserted more easily than a whole piece. **Edgewise** means "leading with the corner, or edge."

Example:
Mom and Dad, will you please be quiet? I've been trying to tell you why I didn't get home until midnight, but with you screaming at me I **can't get a word in edgewise.**

 not hold water
Be a bad, ineffective argument

Picture it!
A container is a construction. A good container will not let things spill out. If an argument spills, it is useless.

Example:
Professor Dada, your argument that the sun revolves around the earth does **not hold water.**

AN ARGUMENT IS A BATTLE

 stick to your guns
Hold your position in the face of strong opposition

Picture it!
If argument is battle, then continuing to shoot when being shot at is like continuing to support an idea while contrary ideas are being expressed. This metaphor is consistent with the basic metaphor *Ideas are sharp instruments* (bullets).

Example:
I know that your family hates your idea of moving to Arizona, but you should **stick to your guns.** It's easier to buy a house there.

 shoot down
Destroy

Picture it!
If an argument is a vehicle—let's say, a plane—then shooting down the plane is destroying the argument.

Example:
I'm glad you **shot down** Professor Dada's contention that the sun revolves around the earth. The man is completely crazy.

 duck the issue
Avoid dealing with, or arguing about, an issue

Picture it!
To duck is to bend at the knees to avoid being hit. To avoid being hit by a thrown object is like avoiding an argument.

Example:
The president of the company isn't saying anything about the lawsuit. At the news conference yesterday, he **ducked the issue** entirely.

 take flak (for)
Receive criticism or angry arguments against

Picture it!
Flak consists of exploding shells fired at an aircraft. Your argument can be attacked, just as a plane can.

Example:
Peter suggested that we hold class outside today. He sure **took a lot of flak** from Professor Davis for that idea!

Understanding and Using Idioms

Complete the sentences with idioms from the list.

jump on the bandwagon	*switch gears*	*get sidetracked*
get a word in edgewise	*on shaky ground*	*duck the issue*
let me put it this way	*don't hold water*	*shot down*
stuck to my guns	*take flak for*	*jump in*

Professor Wise Lectures on Guns In Contemporary America

As many of you know, the NRA —National Rifle Association— has a lot of power, but their arguments in favor of handguns just _____₁_____. Their motto seems to be, "A chicken in every pot, a car in every garage, and a gun in every hand," but this is a recipe for social disaster. _____₂_____: if everyone has a gun, many thousands more will be shot every year.

Now, if some of you have opinions or questions, feel free to _____₃_____ whenever you want. This is meant to be an open discussion. And in that spirit of openness, let me tell you about my experience in Washington, when I was an

advisor to President Simon. And, by the way, I played baseball with Simon when we were in college, but I suppose that is beside the point, and I don't want to _____. So, back to the NRA and my time in the capital.
₄

Those NRA representatives were part of every discussion about guns. I tried to express my opinions, but I couldn't _____. They monopolized the discussion. Finally, the president had to ask my opinion. Well, I _____ the NRA arguments, one by one. Of course, that was easy, because they were _____ to start with. And though they fired questions at me for a half hour, I _____. And by the time it was over, it was clear that they were dead ducks.

Of course, the president knew that if he turned against the NRA, he would _____ it. I mean, he would get thousands of angry letters from gun owners who want their automatic rifles to shoot deer. So, in the end, what he did was to _____. He said that Congress should act on gun control, that it was not his job to speak for the American people.

Now, I'd like to _____ and talk about how money influences political decisions. The sad fact is that the NRA gives money to senators who then vote against gun control. And when it becomes obvious that the NRA is going to win, the previously indecisive senators _____ and vote against gun control like the majority of others.

Conversation Questions

Pair Work. Ask each other the following questions. If your partner asks for additional information, use your imagination to think of something. If you hear a very interesting response, share it with the class.

1. Tell me about some decision you made **for** which you **took flak**. Or tell me about some decision **for** which you did not **take flak** even though you probably should have.

2. If I decided to run for president of my country, would you **jump on the bandwagon?** Why or why not?

3. My boyfriend/girlfriend told me I should always pay for our dates because I have ten thousand dollars in the bank. I told him/her I wouldn't, and now he/she is threatening to leave me. Should I **stick to my guns?** Why or why not?

4. My girlfriend/boyfriend thinks we should get married. Do you think I should **duck the issue** or confront it?

5. There is a student in my English class who talks so much no one can **get a word in edgewise.** Do you think I should say something to him or to the teacher?

6. I told my friend, who has a nine-month-old baby, that I should be able to say anything I want in the kid's presence, even bad words. He said my argument did **not hold water.** I said it held more water than his kid did. What do you think? Does my argument **hold water?**

7. Have you had any teachers who **got sidetracked** easily? If so, tell me about them.

8. My mother says that women are more sensitive than men. Is she **on shaky ground** with that opinion?

9. If I said that the lost continent of Atlantis had a very advanced civilization ten thousand years ago, do you think the class would **shoot me down?** Explain.

Understanding, Speaking, and Writing

Write a conversation between two students, Thelma and Ellen. For each speech, read the description of what the student wants to say, then transform that information into one or more sentences, replacing each italicized phrase with an idiom. You must write out the entire speech, not just the idiom. Read the conversation with a partner, each partner taking one role. Then switch roles and read the conversation a second time. (Note: to *assent* is to say words like *yeah, yes, OK, hmm, all right,* or *right.*)

Thelma asks Ellen if she went to the lecture that day.

Thelma: _____

_____

Ellen did, but she wishes Professor Wise would organize his lectures better. Just when he gets to the heart of the issue he *digresses* to a new topic.

Ellen: _____

_____

Thelma knows what Ellen means. But the problem is not just Wise. Every time a discussion gets going, the kid with the big mouth *enters the discussion* and no one can *speak because he won't shut up.*

Thelma: _____

_____

Ellen assents. The kid's arguments *are bad and ineffective. She wants to express her argument in this way:* if he had a brain he would be dangerous.

Ellen: _____

_____

Thelma is looking forward to writing evaluations of the class. Professor Wise is really going to *take some criticism*.

Thelma: _____

_____

Ellen assents. But she is going to praise him for his brave stance on gun control. At least he doesn't *avoid the issue*.

Ellen: _____

_____

Creative Conversation

Complete the conversation, using the numbered hints. Read the conversation twice with a partner, changing roles the second time. Do not look at your partner's text. You must remember how your partner filled in the blanks so that you can respond in an appropriate way.

1. something George never does but is supposed to do (take out the garbage)
2. year (1985)
3. funny ending to the title (*Goes to Washington, Goes to (some place), Lectures on Einstein*)
4. room in the house (living room)

Martha: George, I want to talk seriously about the problems in our relationship. One problem is that you never _____.
                                                                    1

George: What do you mean I never _____? You're **on shaky**
                                       1
ground there, darling. I always _____.
                                    1
The real problem in our relationship is that I **can't get a word in edgewise.**

Martha: There you go again, George, **ducking the issue.** And it isn't true that I talk too much. I just **stick to my guns** when I have an opinion, which is something you never have. When was the last time you read a real book? _____?
            2

George: Very funny, Martha. But that does**n't hold water.** I just read a book last week.

Martha: Right. I remember. It was *Mickey Mouse* _____.
                                                      3

George: Well, at least it's better than that psychological nonsense you read. Every time a new idea comes out you just **jump on the bandwagon.** But let me tell you something, sweetie, that wagon isn't rolling in my

_____ anymore.
     4

Sentence Completion

Finish the sentences.

1. "Let's not **get sidetracked** by the issue of taxes," the president said to the press. "The real problem now is _____

_____.

2. Maybe you didn't understand when I said that your paper on Plato was not as good as it could be. **Let me put it this way,** your paper _____

_____.

3. We've been discussing the art of western, or cowboy, movies. Let's **switch gears** and _____

_____.

4. Everybody is making science-fiction films these days, but I refuse to **jump on the bandwagon.** I'm going to _____

_____.

5. If anybody wants to **jump in,** _____

_____.

6. You would be **on shaky ground** if you insisted that _____

_____.

7. At home I **can't get a word in edgewise** because _____

_____.

8. Your argument that _____

does **not hold water.** And I'll tell you why. First, _____

_____.

9. All I said was that pizza was the most nutritious food, and all these food

    experts **shot me down.** They said _____

    _____ .

10. I think that _____ (country) will **stick to its guns** on the

    issue of _____

    because _____

    _____ .

11. The president of _____ (country) **ducked the issue** of

    _____

    because _____

    _____ .

12. The president will **take a lot of flak** if he says _____

    _____ .

Writing and Speaking

Write six Conversation Questions similar to the ones on pages 46–47, using idioms from this chapter. Then ask and answer these new questions with a partner.

1. _____

   _____

2. _____

   _____

3. _____

   _____

4. _____

   _____

5. _____

   _____

6. _____

   _____

American Art 101

Look at the painting *Baptism in Kansas* (1928) by John Steuart Curry and use five idioms from this chapter to tell what is happening in the painting, or how you feel about the painting, or what one of the people in the painting might say.

Example: Anyone who thinks that baptisms in Kansas were not dramatic would be on very shaky ground.

1. _____

   _____

2. _____

   _____

3. _____

   _____

4. _____

   _____

5. _____

   _____

Rewriting Using Idioms

Rewrite the following piece of art criticism, using idioms from this chapter and preserving the sense of the passage. You will have to do more than simply substitute phrases: sometimes you will have to change the structure of the sentence.

Although John Steuart Curry was interested in social justice, he thought it was too easy for painters to *digress into* fashionable political language, which was changing day by day. *Expressing the argument this way:* he was more concerned with what he felt were lasting issues. His moralism was old-fashioned. He did not *follow the contemporary political movement.* He *received strong criticism* from very political artists for *avoiding dealing with* the issue of class struggle, but in truth he was more interested in farmers' struggles with tornadoes, storms, and other destructive forces of nature. Curry *held his artistic position in the face of strong opposition,* recording social events in rural America with wonderful details.

Presentation

Prepare a short presentation (up to five minutes) to the class on any topic you wish. Use as many of the idioms in this chapter as you feel comfortable with.

Suggested Topics

Gun control in the United States

Why people should (should not)
    be allowed to carry guns in
        _____ (name of
    country)

Regulations on possessing guns in your
    country

Why _____ (name
    of country) is becoming more/less
    dangerous

chapter 5

BASIC METAPHORS
- Emotions Are a Force
- Emotional Trauma Is a Storm
- Extreme Emotion Is Death
- Anger Is Explosion
- Emotional Normalcy Is Togetherness

INTRODUCTION   The idea shared by the basic metaphors in this unit is that emotions are a force, and the force is often destructive. We speak of emotions in terms of storms, explosions, death, and lack of togetherness. Other languages have similar metaphors for emotions. Reason is calm and cool, while emotions are hot and violent.

WARM-UP   In your native language, what does it mean for a person to be *hot* or *cold?* Now make a short list of emotions. In your native language, how are they expressed as a force? Do some emotions push, pull, drive, or explode? Share your answers in groups of three or four.

EMOTIONS ARE A FORCE

 bowl me over
Surprise me, astonish me

Picture it!
Imagine that you are a bowling pin and a bowling ball comes down the alley and knocks you over. Events can have an emotional effect with similar force.

Example:
Winning the Pulitzer Prize for poetry really **bowled me over.**

 strike me (as)
Make an impression on me

Picture it!
To strike is to hit. An event can have a mental or emotional impact that is similar to a physical blow.

Example:
The Eiffel Tower in France **struck me as** great architecture.

 knock me out / a knockout
Amaze me with quality / very attractive woman; terrific thing

Picture it!
In boxing, to knock someone out is to hit him so hard he loses consciousness. Anything with exceptional quality or exceptional beauty has similar force.

Example:
Perlman's performance of Mozart's violin concerto really **knocked me out.**
(**Note:** *Knockout can be used as an adjective.*)

 floor me
Amaze or shock me

Picture it!
To floor someone is to hit him or her so hard he or she falls to the floor. This is very similar to a knockout.

Example:
My father was **floored** when I got my grades. They were all A's.

EMOTIONAL TRAUMA IS A STORM

 weather the storm
Survive difficulties

Picture it!
The emotional trauma is a storm. *To weather* means "to endure."

Example:
The president was upset at the numerous scandals in his administration, but he **weathered the storm.**

 blow over
Pass (said of some turmoil)

Picture it!
Storms are difficult to endure, but they pass, and good weather returns.

Example:
You are feeling bad about your divorce, but it will all **blow over.**

 blow me away
Impress me greatly

Picture it!
The event is a storm. It is so strong that it affects the mind.

Example:
Your garden is so beautiful. It **blows me away.**

EXTREME EMOTION IS DEATH

 kill me
Make me laugh very hard

Picture it!
You can laugh so hard that it hurts. Death is the extreme logical extension of being hurt.

Example:
That comedian is so funny! She just **kills me.**

 to die for
Very desirable

Picture it!
If you are willing to die for something, it must be very desirable.

Example:
I just love my wife's pancakes. They're **to die for.**

 scare me to death
Scare me very much

Picture it!
The emotion of fright is so strong that it will kill me.

Example:
I saw *Dracula* at the movies and it **scared me to death.**

 dying to
Wanting very much to

Picture it!
If you are willing to die for something, you must want it very much.

Example:
I'm **dying to** take a vacation and play some golf.

ANGER IS EXPLOSION

have a short fuse
Get angry very quickly and easily

Picture it!
A fuse is a stringlike piece that is attached to an explosive. When you light the fuse, it burns until it reaches the explosive. If the fuse is short, the explosion will come quickly.

Example:
My father **has a short fuse.** All I did was tell him that I *might* get a C in English and he screamed at me and took away my TV.

blow off some steam
Let some anger come out (for example, by shouting), preventing a disastrous explosion later on

Picture it!
If you boil water in a pressure cooker, it can explode. You prevent the disastrous explosion by opening a valve and letting some steam (water in gaseous state) blow off.

Example:
Son, I'm sorry I yelled at you for getting a C. I was just **blowing off some steam.** If I had held it in, who knows what I might have done.

blow up
Become very angry

Picture it!
When a person shouts with anger, it is like an explosion.

Example:
When the chef saw that his main course had been burned, he **blew up.**

EMOTIONAL NORMALCY IS TOGETHERNESS

15 **pull yourself together**
To return to emotional normalcy

Picture it!
During emotional trauma, people act as if they are no longer in their normal state. Pulling oneself together returns one to that normal state.

Example:
My brother cried when it was announced that he had won the Academy Award, but he **pulled himself together** and accepted the award.

16 **come apart at the seams**
Become emotionally unstable because of some trauma

Picture it!
A seam is the place where one piece of cloth or material is sewn or attached to another.

If the seam comes apart, then the insides will come out. If a person comes apart at the seams, the person is out of control.

 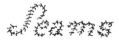

Example:
When Roy's horse died, it was a terrible time for him. Roy was **coming apart at the seams.** He had ridden that old horse for twenty years and had never had another horse.

17 **fall apart**
Become emotionally unstable, unable to function normally

Picture it!
Wholeness, or emotional togetherness, is seen as necessary to function normally, to know what we are doing.

Example:
Mr. Gates is **falling apart.** His company just went bankrupt.

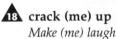

18 crack (me) up
Make (me) laugh

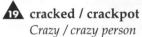

19 cracked / crackpot
Crazy / crazy person

Picture it!
Some things develop cracks before they fall apart. When I laugh very hard, I feel as if my body is going to explode, so if my face were a vase, for example, it would develop cracks.

Picture it!
If you drop a pot or some other fragile object and crack it, it is no longer in a useful, normal state.

Example:
Every time he tells that story about his dog he **cracks me up.**

Examples:
George is **cracked.** He thinks he's Superman, and he's going to jump off the roof.
The **crackpot** dictator just declared war on France.

Understanding and Using Idioms

Complete the sentences with idioms from the list.

weathered the storm	*kills me*	*cracked*
pull yourselves together	*crackpot*	*bowled*
blow off some steam	*falls apart*	*blew up*
having short fuses	*knockout*	*dying to*
blow you away	*crack you up*	*floored*
scared to death	*to die for*	*blow over*
come apart at the seams		

Professor Wadkins Lectures on Sex, Genes, and Viruses

I see that many of you undergraduates are wearing baseball hats. Well, hold on to

your hats, because my lecture today may _____. I know you're
                                              1

_____ hear it, because of the first word of the lecture title. But the
        2

"s" word is the least important of the three words.

Not only will you think that I have deceived you, but you will also think that I

am _____ when I tell you that all we really are, as human beings, is
        3

a colony of viruses! That's right! Essentially, we are a colony of viruses. I see

some of you removing those baseball hats you wear all the time to scratch your

heads—for viruses, no doubt. . . . OK, well, that joke was supposed to

_____, but the lack of laughter indicates that you are a tough
        4

audience. Not that I haven't faced tough audiences before—I have

_____ of criticism and scorn from colleagues at conferences all
        5

over the world, even when I have given a _____ lecture. And
                                          6

some of my associates are famous for _____. They just
                                        7

_____ when they heard my theories.
        8

Now, the point is this: viruses are just genes that have broken free of colonies

such as ourselves. So our genes are colonies of mutated viruses! Some students

_____ when they hear that.
        9

Now, how does sex get into this? Well, what good is sex, anyway? You're

all shaking your heads again, thinking, "Old Professor Wadkins, that

_____—he doesn't know that good sex is like a good apple
        10

tart—it's _____." Just ask the male praying mantis*—he gets eaten
            11

by his mate after sex.

Sex is just a way for our genes to replicate. They—our genes—are the boss. "We"

are a fiction! That just _____! We are a cosmic joke—we think we
                          12

are masters of the universe, but we are just a colony of parasitic† viruses called

genes! I myself was _____ over when I realized that.
                      13

How did this come about? It's just like a big corporation, which was formed by

merging many small businesses. Frightening? A bit, I suppose, but should we really

be _____ to think that a human being, then, is a business of sorts?
      14

Think of the relationship of a parasite and its host. They live off each other.

Then one day they realize they might as well merge—become one creature! Some

virus was parasitic to a cell for millennia, then became part of it and became

known as a gene.

* *praying mantis: insect similar to a big grasshopper*
† *parasitic: living off another creature*

Well, that's it for today. If you're as _____ by all this as I was
15
when I discovered it, I hope you can _____ by Thursday. And if
16
you want to _____ about these theories that challenge your sense
17
of identity or about your grade on last Friday's test, stop by my office this
afternoon.

I hope that nobody _____ and has to take antidepressant drugs
18
after getting the results. And even if your parents are mad, just take it easy. It will
all _____ by Christmas.
19

Conversation Questions

Pair Work. Ask each other the following questions. If your partner asks for additional
information, use your imagination to think of something. If you hear a very interesting
response, share it with the class.

1. When was the last time there was an economic crisis in your country, and how did people **weather the storm?**

2. The furnace in my apartment makes loud noises at night. I complained to the landlord, but he hasn't done anything. I'm sure he thinks it will all **blow over.** What should I do now? Just let it **blow over?**

3. I was **blown away** when I heard about mad cow disease. How about you? Do you know about it? Does it **blow you away?**

4. I have a friend who just **kills** me. Every time he opens his mouth, I laugh. How about you? Is there anyone who does that to you?

5. Tell me something that really **scares you to death.**

6. Is there some actress that you consider a **knockout?**

7. Tell me something you're **dying to** do or something you're **dying to** tell somebody.

8. When is the last time you really **blew up?** Why?

9. Who do you know who really **has a short fuse?**

10. OK, this is your big opportunity to **blow off some steam.** So tell me what's on your mind. What do you want to **blow off steam** about?

11. My girlfriend/boyfriend and I broke up yesterday and I feel terrible. I don't have much experience with this. How long do you think it will take me to **pull myself together?**

12. Do you know anyone you'd describe as **coming apart at the seams?** Why?

13. My brother is **falling apart.** Since his wife left him, he's been gambling more. His debts keep increasing, and he doesn't have the cash to pay them. Some bad men are threatening him. What should I advise him to do?

14. Is there a comedian who really **cracks you up?** Or a TV show? Who or what? Why?

15. Every family and every neighborhood seems to have at least one member who is **cracked,** just as every country seems to have at least one politician who is **cracked.** Tell me about some **crackpot.**

16. Is there anybody who **strikes you as** almost saintly?

17. Would you be **floored** if your best friend came home with a tattoo?

18. Tell me about some food that is **to die for.**

Understanding and Speaking

Pair Work. Complete the conversation with the idioms in the list. Read the conversation with a partner, and then switch roles and read it again.

blowing off some steam	*crackpot*	*blew up*
pulls himself together	*crack me up*	*dying to*
scared me to death	*blew me away*	*kill*

Bart: Professor Wadkins!

Wadkins: Goodness! You almost _____! Don't scream like
            ₁
            that! My heart can't take it.

Bart: Sorry, but you said we could see you after class, and I've been

            _____ ask you a couple of questions. I mean, like,
            ₂
            last week you said computers can think, right?

Wadkins: Yes.

Bart: Well, that _____. And I started thinking—how
            ₃
            about a thermostat*? Does it think too?

Wadkins: Of course. Better than you, judging from your last test.

Bart: Yeah, well, excuse me for _____, but the test
            ₄
            revealed some prejudice on your part.

Wadkins: Yes, prejudice for intelligent students.

Bart: Ha! Professor, you _____. But speaking of
            ₅
            prejudice, my friend Rashid really _____ when I
            ₆
            told him your theory that racial prejudice was just a rational generalization

            of a tendency to identify with individuals who resemble you.

* *thermostat: device that senses temperature and makes the heat go on or off automatically*

Wadkins: Well, when your friend _____ he can find comfort

                 ₇
in the widespread opinion that I'm a _____.

                 ₈

Bart: Professor, you just _____ me. I don't believe half

                 ₉
of what you teach, but your sense of humor is really cool.

Creative Conversation

Complete the conversation, using the numbered hints. Read the conversation twice with a partner, changing roles the second time. Do not look at your partner's text. You must remember how your partner filled in the blanks so that you can respond in an appropriate way.

1. something one could leave on (stove, water)

2. reason George left number 1 on (if "stove," then "cooking such a nice soup"; if "water," then "washing the . . .")

3. a holiday

4. a relative (father, aunt)

5. a dish (stuffed peppers, sushi)

6. description of another article of clothing (red-and-white striped tie)

Martha: George, you left the _____ on again!

                 ₁

George: Well, turn it off, for goodness sake! I mean, instead of **blowing up,** you
might thank me for _____.

                 ₂

Martha: Oh, you just **kill** me. You do something wrong, and somehow I'm the
one to blame. You really **crack me up.**

George: My love, **pull yourself together.** It's _____, and

                 ₃
we're going to your _____'s for dinner. And I love

                 ₄
your _____'s _____. It's **to**

      ₄   ₅
die for.

Martha: Who are you kidding, George? Last year you said you nearly died *from*
it. And talk about **a short fuse**—all my _____ did

                 ₄
was mention that your purple checked pants didn't go with your
_____, and you almost **came apart at the seams.**

                 ₆

George: It just **blows me away** that you could misinterpret me so badly. I was
just **blowing off a little steam.** The holidays always have that effect on me.

Sentence Completion

Finish these sentences.

1. Many people think that _____ is a **knockout** because

_____.

2. I was really **bowled over** by the fact that _____

_____.

3. War **strikes me as** _____

_____.

4. One disastrous event in my country was _____. The

   people were able to **weather the storm** because _____

_____.

5. One thing that **blows me away** about _____ (name of a

   country, city, or institution) is that _____

_____.

6. My friend was accused of cheating on an exam, but I think it will all **blow over**

   because _____

_____.

7. Every time he _____, it just **kills me.**

8. Man, I was just **scared to death** when _____

_____.

9. _____ is **to die for.** I mean, _____

_____.

10. What I am **dying to** do is _____ because _____

_____.

11. _____ **blows up** when _____

_____.

12. I hate arguing with _____ because he/she has such a

    short fuse. I mean, one time _____

_____.

13. Do you mind if I **blow off some steam** about _____?

What bothers me is _____

_____.

14. _____ suffered serious trauma when _____,

but he/she **pulled himself/herself together** and _____

_____.

15. One person who I think will never **come apart at the seams** is _____

_____. The reason I say that is _____

_____.

16. The most common reason for people under thirty **falling apart** is probably

_____.

17. I'm going to tell you a joke that will really **crack you up.** _____

_____.

18. _____ is really **cracked.** One thing he/she does/did is

_____.

19. My father was really **floored** when _____

_____.

Writing and Speaking

Write six Conversation Questions similar to the ones on pages 61–62, using idioms from this chapter. Then ask and answer these new questions with a partner.

1. _____

_____

2. _____

_____

3. _____

_____

4. _____

_____

5. _____

_____

6. _____

_____

American Art 101

Look at the painting *American Gothic* (1930) by Grant Wood and use five idioms from this chapter to tell what is happening in the painting, or how you feel about the painting, or what one of the people in the painting might say.

Example: I'd love to invite this couple to a party. They would really crack everybody up.

1. _____

   _____

2. _____

   _____

3. _____

   _____

4. _____

   _____

5. _____

   _____

Rewriting Using Idioms

Rewrite the following piece of art criticism, using idioms from this chapter and preserving the sense of the passage. You will have to do more than simply substitute phrases for the italicized words: sometimes you will have to change the structure of the sentence.

Grant Wood's "American Gothic" is one of America's most famous paintings. When it was first exhibited, in 1930, it *impressed audiences greatly*. People were *wanting very much* to see it. This was a time when Americans began to have renewed respect for their national heritage.

Look at this couple—don't they just *make you laugh hard*? They appear to have *survived some difficulties*. Indeed, most farmers in the Midwest did. Their lives were hard. They all endured trauma from natural disasters and had to *return to emotional normalcy* more than once.

During the 1920s, Wood traveled to Germany to study painting, and the Daughters of the American Revolution, a conservative group, *let some anger come out* about Wood's visiting the land of the First World War enemy. One wonders if "American Gothic" is Wood's revenge against such conservative groups: is Wood making fun of the values of this old-fashioned couple?

Presentation

Prepare a short presentation (up to five minutes) to the class on any topic you wish. Use as many of the idioms in this chapter as you feel comfortable with.

Suggested Topics

Some disease that we now have, or soon may have, a cure for

Some medical problem that could be cured if the government would spend some money on it

Conservative groups in your country

An artist you like

chapter 6

> **BASIC METAPHORS**
> • Money Is Blood
> • Money Is Food

INTRODUCTION   All money is symbolic. Even gold has very limited use. Its use-fulness cannot justify its value to us. And your paper dollar? It might be useful for starting a fire, but for little else. Your paper dollar is a symbol: it represents a small amount of gold. And that gold symbolizes purchasing power. The symbolism extends to the way money is spoken of idiomatically. Because money is valuable and basic, we refer to it with idioms that include valuable and basic things. So it should be no surprise that English exhibits the basic metaphors *Money is blood* and *Money is food.*

WARM-UP   In your native language, how is money referred to in slang? Is it referred to in terms of valuable or basic things? Share your answers with a group of three or four.

MONEY IS BLOOD

1 **be in the red**
Have a negative balance sheet, where more money has been spent than earned

Picture it!
It is traditional accounting practice that when expenses are greater than income, the result is written in red ink. Red is the color of blood, and for some people losing money is like losing blood.

Example:
My parents' business is $100,000 **in the red,** and they said we're taking a long vacation but they won't say where.

 make a killing (in)
Make a huge profit investing (in)

Picture it!
If money is blood, then killing can produce a lot of money, since it can produce a lot of blood.

Example:
My uncle **made a killing** in oil.

 to mean business
To be very serious, almost threatening

Picture it!
If money is blood, and business is associated with money, then *to mean business* is to imply some risk of losing blood, which is serious, even threatening.

Example:
I'm really tired of complaining to you about your dog barking all night. This time I **mean business.**

 cut/slash prices
To reduce prices, often substantially

Picture it!
To slash is to cut with the edge of a knife or sword, using a swinging motion. To slash prices is to lose profits, the same way you would lose blood if you slashed your arm.

Example:
Some computer makers have **cut the prices** of personal computers by 90 percent.

 pay through the nose
Pay an extremely high price

Picture it!
Many people experience nosebleeds. One way to dramatize paying an extremely high price is to compare it to losing valuable blood from your nose.

Example:
If you want one of those new TVs with a large screen and an excellent picture, you have to **pay through the nose.**

 cut-throat
Tough, extreme (said of things like competition)

Picture it!
To cut someone's throat almost inevitably causes death. Competition can be so extreme that it is similar to cutting someone's throat, which leads to blood—which is money.

Example:
My father used to sell used cars, but he got out of the business because it was so **cut-throat.**

MONEY IS FOOD

 dough
Money

Picture it!
Dough is a mixture of flour, water, and yeast. Dough is what bread is made from. Dough, which is considered elementary for survival, symbolizes money, which is also seen as elementary for survival.
(**Note:** *Bread also can mean money.*)

Example:
Boy: Please, Mister, I lost my money and this is the last bus and it's getting dark. Can I get on?
Bus Driver: Sorry, kid. No **dough,** no go.

reap the benefits/profits
Benefit, profit

Picture it!
To reap is to harvest a crop, such as wheat. Benefits or profits are a form of money and are seen as the crop one cuts down and gathers.

Example:
The company spent a lot of money on new computers, and now it is **reaping the benefits.**

9 **be peanuts / for peanuts**
Be / for a very small amount of money

Picture it!
In the United States, you can buy lots of peanuts for a dollar, so each peanut is worth very little.

Example:
I'm glad that you worked hard all summer selling lemonade and saved five hundred dollars, but, to be honest, that's **peanuts** when it comes to paying for your college education.

10 **skim (the) profits**
Take a percentage of the profits (illegally or deceptively)

Picture it!
In unhomogenized milk, the cream rises to the top. To skim the cream is to take it off the top of the milk. The cream is the best part. With money that comes into a business, profits are the best part.

Example:
My uncle Mike was caught **skimming the profits** from his movie distribution company.

Understanding and Using Idioms

Complete the sentences with idioms from the list.

make a killing (used twice)	*in the red*	*dough*
skimming the profits	*slash prices*	*reap*
were peanuts	*mean business*	*cut-throat*
pay through the nose		

Professor Friedman Lectures on International Marketing

You might think that corporate executives who are making millions of dollars should be able to avoid the most elementary mistakes in international marketing. But think again. Making a lot of _____ doesn't guarantee wise decision-making. Here are some examples of catastrophically bad marketing, caused by inattention to local language and culture.

In Taiwan, the translation of the Pepsi slogan "Come alive with the Pepsi Generation" came out as "Pepsi will bring your ancestors back from the dead." Pepsi's profits in Taiwan _____ until they realized their error and changed the slogan.
                               2

Kentucky Fried Chicken (KFC) thought they would _____ in China, but their slogan "finger-lickin(g) good" came out as "eat your fingers off."
                                                           3

Hunt-Wesson, who make products like cooking oil and ketchup, introduced their Big John products in Canada as Gros Jos, unaware that it meant "big breasts." In this case, however, there was no noticeable effect on sales. Unlike KFC, they did not have to _____ to keep business going. Their ketchup sales were
                      4
poor, but not _____. Their competitors, however, thought that
                5
Hunt-Wesson was a _____ company. They were outraged that a
                       6
company could _____ profits while lowering public morality
                    7
standards. They thought, "These Hunt-Wesson people really _____."
                                                                        8

And in Miami, a big T-shirt maker printed shirts for the Spanish-speaking market to take advantage of the pope's visit. They thought they would _____ with the T-shirts, and when they didn't, they suspected the
           9
vendors who worked for the company of _____. But when they
                                         10
investigated the vendors, they found that the T-shirts, which they thought said, "I saw the pope," in fact said, "I saw the potato." And one religious group claimed the T-shirt was disrespectful of the pope and wanted to take the T-shirt maker to court and make the company _____ for their disrespect. The com-
                                       11
pany, however, proved that the T-shirt was just a disastrous mistake.

Conversation Questions

Pair Work. Ask each other the following questions. If your partner asks for additional information, use your imagination to think of something. If you hear a very interesting response, share it with the class.

1. Tell me something you think a business-minded person could **make a killing** in, these days.

2. How do you know when your (father, mother, husband, teacher, or whatever) **means business**? Does he or she have any gestures, a particular tone of voice, or some other way to indicate that he or she **means business**?

3. What do you think is the most **cut-throat** business these days?

4. American Airlines **slashed prices** to win back customers who were worried about a strike. My wife got an incredible fare to Chicago. Have you ever been able to take advantage of **slashed** airline **prices?** Or have you heard of any great deals that you couldn't take advantage of though you wanted to?

5. My sister is always **in the red** because she has twelve credit cards and uses one to pay off the debt on the next, and so on. Do you know anyone **in the red** for similar reasons? What can they do about it?

6. Have you ever had to **pay through the nose** for something? I mean, the price was extremely high but you just had to have the item, so you bought it anyway?

7. What would you do if you found a suitcase filled with **dough,** with nothing to identify the owner?

8. If you really wanted to **reap the benefits** of a college education, where would you go?

9. If I want to go out at night and enjoy myself, I'll make sure I've got about $150 in my wallet. But I hear that for some folks, that**'s peanuts.** Do you know anyone like that? Why might they think that $150 **is peanuts?**

10. My favorite charity received $500,000 more this year than last year. So the head of the charity increased his salary from $100,000 to $150,000. Isn't that just like **skimming the profits?** Do you think it is justifiable?

Understanding and Speaking

Pair Work. Complete the conversation with the idioms in the list. Read the conversation with a partner, and then switch roles and read it again.

making a killing	*in the red*	*dough*
peanuts (used twice)	*cut-throat*	*skim*
slashed		

Holden: My father was one of those guys who were selling "I saw the potato" T-shirts. In fact, I've still got one, but I don't wear it much because some people might think I'm an idiot.

Bart: You are what you are.

Holden: Hey, I got it for _____₁, so I can't be a complete idiot.

Bart: You mean your old man didn't just give it to you?

Holden: What can I say? My old man is a _____₂ businessman.

Bart: I bet he was _____₃ on that deal.

Holden: Yeah. He _____₄ his prices from ten dollars a shirt to two dollars, and he still couldn't sell them. He ended up selling them for

_____5_____. It was so funny! I mean, he was so excited about the pope coming to Miami, but he's not very religious. He was just excited about _____6_____ in pope T-shirts.

Bart: Hey, I've got an idea.

Holden: What?

Bart: I'll bet your old man still has a lot of those T-shirts somewhere, right?

Holden: Yeah. So?

Bart: So, listen. Everyone in our economics class will buy one. We can make enough _____7_____ to pay for spring break in Fort Lauderdale.

Holden: Bart, you're a genius.

Bart: Partners?

Holden: On one condition.

Bart: What?

Holden: You promise that you won't _____8_____ the profits, like the last time we were in business together.

Creative Conversation

Complete the conversation, using the numbered hints. Read the conversation twice with a partner, changing roles the second time. Do not look at your partner's text. You must remember how your partner filled in the blanks so that you can respond in an appropriate way.

1. an instrument that records words or events
2. a relative, family member
3. a number
4. expensive object

5. product one might make money on or area one might make money in
6. object that makes number 4 unnecessary or superfluous
7. name of a sports team
8. number below ten

Sally: Harry, I've got an idea.

Harry: Wait! Let me get the _____1_____ to record this momentous event!

Sally: I'm serious. I have an idea that could make us some real **dough.**

Harry: OK, Sal, you've got that look that says you **mean business.** What's your idea?

Sally: You know all those coffee mugs with designs or artwork on them? Well, we can put a lot of idioms on the mugs, and call them Idiomugs. Everyone would buy one.

Harry: Everyone? I think only your _____ would buy one. Even
2

if we sold _____, what we made would **be peanuts.**
3

I want to buy a _____, and we wouldn't make enough to
4

afford it.

Sally: We'd have to **make a killing** in _____ to afford a
5

_____. Besides, why do you need a _____?
4   4

You already have _____.
6

Harry: The real reason we can't afford a _____ is that we're still
4

in the red from your last great idea—when you decided we could **make a**

killing in _____ hats. You had _____
7   8

thousand hats made, saying "_____: World Champions,"
7

but they didn't win the championship.

Sentence Completion

Finish these sentences.

1. I (don't) think I'll **make a killing** in _____ because

_____

_____.

2. To show a badly disciplined team that he or she **means business,** a coach could

_____

_____.

3. In my country, competition is really **cut-throat** in the area of _____

_____.

4. Last year, coffee producers wanted to **cut prices,** but they couldn't because

_____

_____.

5. Some old state-run enterprises in _____ (country) are

   millions of dollars **in the red,** and I think that the government should _____

   _____ .

6. If you want _____ ,

   you really have to **pay through the nose.**

7. If I had the **dough,** I would _____

   _____ .

8. One way to **reap the benefits** of speaking two languages fluently is to _____

   _____ .

9. If I were a rich and famous singer, I would _____ **for**

   peanuts because _____

   _____ .

10. It might be easy to **skim** the profits from _____ , but I

    would never do it because _____

    _____ .

Writing and Speaking

Write six Conversation Questions similar to the ones on pages 72–73, using idioms from this chapter. Then ask and answer these new questions with a partner.

1. _____

   _____

2. _____

   _____

3. _____

   _____

4. _____

   _____

5. _____

   _____

6. _____

   _____

American Art 101

Look at the painting *Twenty-cent Movie* (1936) by Reginald Marsh and use five idioms from this chapter to tell what is happening in the painting, or how you feel about the painting, or what one of the people in the painting might say.

Example: Fredric March was so popular. They must have had to pay through the nose to get him to star in that old movie.

1. _____

   _____

2. _____

   _____

3. _____

   _____

4. _____

   _____

5. _____

   _____

Rewriting Using Idioms

Rewrite the following piece of art criticism, using idioms from this chapter and preserving the sense of the passage. You will have to do more than simply substitute phrases for the italicized words: sometimes you will have to change the structure of the sentence.

Reginald Marsh was one of the most famous of the Social Realist painters of the 1930s. This was a time when few people had a lot of *money*, but people still managed to entertain themselves with things like movies. Marsh portrayed many facets of life at this time. His paintings show the *extreme* competition, men who *are very serious*, and at the same time carefree people just looking to have a good time, despite the fact that they made a very small amount of *money*.

While many artists *had a negative balance sheet*, some were able to make a living working on government-sponsored art projects, and others, like Marsh, were able to *benefit from* selling their work to wealthy collectors who would *pay an extremely high price* for art either because they loved it or because they believed it would increase in value over the years.

Presentation

Prepare a short presentation (up to five minutes) to the class on any topic you wish. Use as many of the idioms in this chapter as you feel comfortable with.

Suggested Topics

An object or institution that is revered in
   your country

Marketing mistakes

Why _____ (name of a
   product) would not sell well in your
   country

The best-selling _____
   (name of a product) in your country

Products that one has to pay through the
   nose for in your country

---

chapter 7

INTRODUCTION   The association of money and dirt in English is extensive, and that may be surprising, since the United States and England are usually seen as materialistic cultures. The phrase *filthy lucre* ("dirty money") is very old and deeply rooted in our language (the first written use of the phrase was in 1526). And the association of money and bottom/source should be easily understandable: money is the source of so many of our activities, and the source of anything normally has a bottom.

WARM-UP   Think of different ways of cleaning (sweeping, mopping, washing, wiping, and so on). In your native language, can any of these terms be used with money? Share your answers in groups of three or four.

MONEY IS DIRTY

1 clean up
Make a lot of money, often quickly

Picture it!
If money is dirt, then cleaning up gathers all the money together in one place.

Example:
When Mr. Murphy took over as president of the university, he really **cleaned up.** The university agreed to pay him $300,000 a year.

2 money laundering
Making illegally gotten money appear legally earned

Picture it!
Laundering is washing; it removes dirt, which in this case is the dishonest or illegal aspect of its acquisition.

Example:
Some banks in far away places are well known for **money laundering.**

3 take (me) to the cleaners
Take, or cheat me out of, all of my money

Picture it!
Anything taken to the cleaners has its dirt
removed, and the dirt is money.

Example:
My favorite basketball team got **taken to the cleaners** by a star player who got ten million dollars but
did not try very hard.

4 clean out / clean (me) out
Empty something of money / take all my money

Picture it!
To clean something out is to empty it of dirt. If
money is dirty, then cleaning out is removing the
money.

Example:
Samantha **cleaned out** her account and bought a
new BMW.

5 wipe (me) out
*Ruin (me) financially / to destroy something
valuable*

Picture it!
To wipe is to clean up a spill or something dirty. If
my assets are wiped out, something valuable has
been destroyed and I am financially ruined.

Example:
The stock market crash in 1987 **wiped me out.**

7 **moneygrubber / moneygrubbing**
Person for whom making money is everything / accumulating money at the sake of other things

---

Picture it!
To grub is to dig for roots or other things in the dirt.

Example:
How could she have married that man? He's such a **moneygrubber.**

6 **hit pay dirt**
Make a rewarding discovery, find a source of substantial income

---

Picture it!
When you dig for gold and find it, that find is pay dirt.

Example:
Gertrude was always buying cheap art at yard sales. One day she **hit pay dirt.** She bought an old painting of a ship, and later she found out that it was painted by Thomas Eakins, and it was worth a fortune.

8 **filthy rich**
Extremely rich

Picture it!
Filthy means "dirty."

Example:
Donald is **filthy rich.** He's got three BMWs, a Mercedes, and a Rolls.

9 go down the drain / tubes
Be wasted, lose something in which much work was invested

Picture it!
A sink has a drain, which is then connected to tubes (pipes). Dirt and waste go down the drain, then tubes. Your money or your work can do the same thing.

Example:
I had been working on a book on the Cuban revolution for five years, and just when I finished, two other people published best-selling books on it, so all my effort **went down the tubes.**

BOTTOM IS SOURCE (OF MONEY)

10 have deep pockets
Have a vast source of income

Picture it!
The deeper your pockets, the more money they can hold. *Deep* implies going to the bottom—the source.

Example:
Senator May will have no trouble running for reelection since he married a woman with **deep pockets.**

11 foot the bill
Pay the cost of an expensive service or thing

Picture it!
This expression comes from the old sense of *foot*, meaning to add up numbers and put the total at the foot, or bottom, of the page.

Example:
We decided to honeymoon in Belize when my parents said that they would **foot the bill.**

 the bottom line

The final result or position on an issue, the crucial factor

Picture it!

When you do accounting, you add the numbers on all the lines in the income column, then you add the numbers on all the lines in the expense column, and you come up with a final dollar figure—the bottom line, which is the most important number.

Example:

Yesterday Senator Trent said, "**The bottom line** is that we must reform the way we finance elections if we want to preserve democracy."

Understanding and Using Idioms

Complete the sentences with idioms from the list.

hit intellectual pay dirt	*foot the bill*	*clean up*
taken to the cleaners	*money launderers*	*filthy rich*
have deep pockets	*the bottom line*	*wiped out*
go down the drain	*money-grubbing*	*cleaned out*

Professor Touring Lectures on Fibonacci Numbers*

Let me start by warning you that you will never get _____ from
₁

mathematics, but you can _____ and be very satisfied with your
₂

mental discoveries. That's what happened to Leonardo Fibonacci in 1202, when he

investigated how fast rabbits could reproduce in ideal circumstances. Who knows?

Maybe his father raised rabbits in less than ideal circumstances and had his invest-

ment _____. At any rate, Leonardo discovered something phenom-
₃

enal about all of nature.

* *0, 1, 1, 2, 3, 5, 8, 13, 21, 34, 55, 89 . . . (Each number is the sum of the previous two numbers.)*

Suppose you put a newborn pair of rabbits, one male and one female, together. After one month the female becomes sexually mature. There is still one pair. After the second month, the female gives birth to two rabbits, so there are two pairs. The new pair can't reproduce immediately, but the old pair can, so after three months there are three pairs, and so on. Now, since it's important that you retain this, and since I don't want my explanations to —————————————— , let's have a look at a
————4————
rabbit diagram.

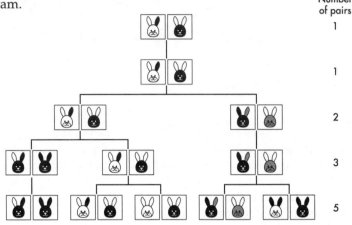

The number of pairs of rabbits each month is 1, 1, 2, 3, 5, 8, 13, 21, 34, . . .

Of course, this is just theoretical. If it were real, your parents could raise rabbits and easily —————————————— for your tuition. And the way costs are rising,
————5————
your parents had better —————————————— . Or they'd better do well in the stock
————6————
market. Indeed, if you could somehow find a Fibonacci series in the stock market, you could really —————————————— , because you could predict the next number
————7————
in the series. And since I was —————————————— by a stockbroker who
————8————
recommended a lot of losers, I'd love to find some correlation myself.

Now, bee reproduction is similar to rabbit reproduction. If you look at a *family tree* of a male worker bee, you will see Fibonacci numbers in the number of parents, grandparents, great-grandparents, etc. And if we take the ratio of any two successive Fibonacci numbers, say, 5/3, 8/5, 13/8, we get, roughly, a number that corresponds to 1.6—which is what the ancient Greeks considered *the golden ratio!*

Say you draw two squares with sides of 1 inch. Now draw another square with sides that are the sum of the previous two, then another square with sides that are the sum of the previous two—you get something like this:

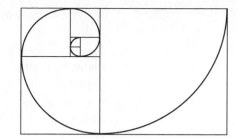

You can see that we can draw a spiral by connecting the squares. This is close to what happens in nature in snail shells and some seashells. Now, you may have noticed that I am trying to make my lecture relevant to you economics majors out there, who form the majority of the class. So, if you were ever completely

_____ , like I was, when you invested in commodities like bananas,
_9_

pineapples, cauliflower, or broccoli, you should know that Fibonacci numbers figure in the way these vegetables and fruits are formed.

And if you are ever digging for flower roots—not _____ but
_10_

knowledge seeking—look at your hands! Two hands, each of which has five fingers, each of which has three parts, separated by two knuckles . . . !

_____ , in my mind, is that God must be a mathematician!
_11_

And just one materialistic anecdote, to conclude: the FBI recently discovered illegal accounts in banks in the Cayman Islands. The FBI agents knew that the

_____ who created the accounts liked to identify them with long
_12_

Fibonacci numbers like 1597 4181, so it was easy to pick out the hidden accounts.

Conversation Questions

Pair Work. Ask each other the following questions. If your partner asks for additional information, use your imagination to think of something. If you hear a very interesting response, share it with the class.

1. My neighbors Jill and Jack are always fighting and threatening each other with divorce. They have a joint bank account, and Jill is worried that Jack will **clean out** the account and disappear. What should she do?

2. If you were going to gamble and you really wanted to **clean up,** what form of gambling would you choose?

3. Have you or your parents or anyone you know been **taken to the cleaners?** Describe what happened.

4. Do you know anything about **money laundering?** Like who does it or where it is done?

5. Last year my computer crashed. I mean, it just gave me nonsense symbols instead of letters. All my valuable files were **wiped out.** Has that ever happened to you or anyone you know?

6. Is there anyone you know or have heard about whom you would consider to be a **moneygrubber?**

7. Do you know anyone who is **filthy rich?** And does it bother you that some people are **filthy rich** while others are starving? Is that just the way the world is, or can anything be done about it, realistically speaking?

8. Some virus researchers think they have **hit pay dirt.** In Norway, seven bodies seem to be frozen, so the 1918 flu virus that killed them may still be alive and can be studied. Can you think of any reason why this might not prove to be **pay dirt?**

9. I trained for several months for this boxing match, then just before the match I twisted my ankle and couldn't fight, so all my work **went down the tubes.** Has anything like this ever happened to you?

10. What advice would you give to young parents who will have to **foot the bill** for their children's college education in fifteen or so years?

11. If you had a relative with **deep pockets,** would you ever ask him or her for a favor or a loan? Under what circumstances might you do so?

12. My aunt and uncle have a ten-year-old daughter who wants to be a gymnast. She wants to compete in the Olympic Games someday, so she spends all her time in the gym, doesn't do any homework, and doesn't read any books. What's **the bottom line** here, for my aunt and uncle? What restrictions should they put on the girl?

Understanding, Speaking, and Writing

Write a conversation between two students, Thelma and Ellen. For each speech, read the description of what the student wants to say, then transform that information into one or more sentences, replacing each italicized phrase with an idiom. You must write out the entire speech, not just the idiom. Read the conversation with a partner, each partner taking one role. Then switch roles and read the conversation a second time.

Thelma is tired of not being able to buy both a hamburger and french fries. She is thinking of becoming, upon graduation, a stockbroker *who is devoted to making money.*

Thelma: _____

_____

_____

(in a sarcastic, joking manner) If Thelma is going to become completely materialistic, she should go into *the business of making illegal money look legal,* which will make her *extremely wealthy.*

Ellen: _____

_____

_____

For Thelma, *the crucial factor* is that she cannot break the law. But the suggestion makes her think that Professor Touring probably uses a Fibonacci number as his password for his computer link to the college.

Thelma: _____

_____

_____

(Thelma sits at her computer and tries different Fibonacci passwords.)

Ellen wants to know why Thelma is doing this. Does she want to *empty* his bank account?

Ellen: _____

_____

_____

Thelma has *made a rewarding discovery!* She now can access her grades and change them from failing to 89s. That is a Fibonacci number, so Professor Touring will not suspect anything.

Thelma: _____

_____

_____

Ellen feels it is necessary to warn Thelma that if college officials find out, her three years at Harvey College will *be wasted*, since she'll get kicked out.

Ellen: _____

_____

_____

Thelma agrees. She won't change anything.

Thelma: _____

_____

_____

Creative Conversation

Complete the conversation, using the numbered hints. Read the conversation twice with a partner, changing roles the second time. Do not look at your partner's text. You must remember how your partner filled in the blanks so that you can respond in an appropriate way.

1. name of a street
2. amount of money one might pay for a decent used car
3. brand of car
4. relative or family member

5. describe what went wrong with the car
6. name of girl
7. telephone number
8. coin one would use for a telephone call

Bart: I've got to buy a used car so I can live off campus. There are some cheap

apartments on _____ Street. But I'm afraid the car
                          1

would **wipe out** my savings.

Thelma: How much are we talking about here, _____?
                                                    2

You can get a decent used _____ for that. You
                                3

don't have to be **filthy rich,** unless you want a BMW.

Bart: I'd never buy a _____. My _____
                            3   4

bought one once, and _____.
                            5

Thelma: OK. Buy a lottery ticket. Maybe you'll **hit pay dirt** and you can get

the BMW. Either that or marry some girl with **deep pockets,** like

_____.
       6

Bart: Hey, Thelma, do you think I'm a **moneygrubber?**

Thelma: No comment on that. But I do want to warn you that you can get **taken
to the cleaners** by used-car salesmen. So you should have a mechanic
check out any car before you buy it.

Bart: Well, **the bottom line** is that I've got to live off campus, and that means

getting a car. So, do you have _____'s phone number?
                                      6

Thelma: Yeah, Mr. **Moneygrubber.** It's _____.
                                               7

Bart: _____. Thanks. And, uh, can I borrow a
              7

_____ for the phone?
          8

Sentence Completion

Finish these sentences.

1. _____ was playing cards with _____,

   and they **cleaned him/her out** so badly that _____

   _____.

2. My friend got a job with _____. She really **cleaned up.** I

   mean, they gave her _____

   _____.

3. I bought this old _____ that I thought was still good, but I

   was **taken to the cleaners!** I mean, _____

   _____.

4. Sometimes legitimate banks get involved in **money laundering** because _____

   _____.

5. If I made a bad investment in _____ and I got **wiped out,**

   I would _____

   _____.

6. I dislike **moneygrubbing** people who _____

   _____.

7. If I were **filthy rich,** _____

   _____.

8. The authorities investigating _____ **hit pay dirt** when __

   _____.

9. All her efforts **went down the tubes** when _____

   _____.

10. I hope _____ will **foot the bill** for _____,

    because _____

    _____.

11. _____ **has deep pockets,** but _____

    _____.

12. People talk a lot about making peace in _____, but **the**

bottom line is that _____

_____.

_____

Writing and Speaking

Write six Conversation Questions similar to the ones on pages 85–86, using idioms from this chapter. Then ask and answer these new questions with a partner.

1. _____

2. _____

_____

3. _____

_____

4. _____

_____

5. _____

_____

6. _____

_____

Presentation

Prepare a short presentation (up to five minutes) to the class on any topic you wish. Use as many of the idioms in this chapter as you feel comfortable with.

Suggested Topics

How to buy a used car

Social justice and the filthy rich

How the economy will be different in
    twenty years

Raising rabbits (or chickens, or other animals)

Fibonacci numbers, or some other interest-
    ing mathematical discovery

chapter 8

BASIC METAPHORS
- Control Is Contact
- Control Is Hand Contact
- Control Is Contact via Strings

INTRODUCTION   Metaphors tend to express the difficult in terms of the simple, the abstract in terms of the physical. Therefore, metaphors help us to understand.

We can control people and things in many different ways, but the most basic way is by physical contact, especially hand contact. Hence the basic metaphors: *Control is contact* and *Control is hand contact.*

Perhaps one of the earliest inventions was string, which was used to control animals. Out of this arose our basic metaphor: *Control is contact via strings. (Note:* The idioms in this category include rope and other things that are stringlike.)

WARM-UP   Think of different ways that a person could be attached by strings, rope, or similar things. In your native language, are there any expressions that represent control of a person by these things? Share your expressions with a group of three or four.

CONTROL IS CONTACT

 up in the air
Unsettled, having an uncertain outcome

Picture it!
A thing floating in the air, like a balloon, normally has no contact with the ground. It moves with the air currents. We don't know where it will go, and we can't control it. (This idiom may refer to a person or a thing.)

Example:
Congress may raise taxes or cut them this year. It's still **up in the air.**

 pin him down
Force him to make precise, unambiguous statements

Picture it!
Imagine a butterfly flying in its unpredictable pattern. If the meaning of a person's statement is like that, you cannot grasp it. If you pin the butterfly to a piece of wood, you control its movements.

Example:
The president said he wants to provide free health care for those who really need it, but whom does that include? Reporters should **pin him down.**

 fly off the handle
Get excessively angry, lose one's temper

Picture it!
You move many objects by means of a handle. When the object becomes detached from the handle while being moved, you are no longer in control of that object.

Example:
I'm sorry I **flew off the handle** last night. I really didn't mean those things I said.

get carried away
Do something to excess, be extremely excited

Picture it!
If you are carried away, you are no longer in control of your movements. Your enthusiasm for what you are doing can get so strong that it carries you away, and you do it to excess.

Example:
My friend says she is writing a historical novel, but she has **gotten so carried away** with research that she hasn't written a word.

CONTROL IS HAND CONTACT

 get ahold of yourself
Control your emotions

Picture it!
When you get ahold of something, you establish firm contact with it, using your hands.

Example:
Get ahold of yourself, Denise. You can't scream at the referee every time he makes a call against your team.

 out of my hands
Outside of my personal control (said of a matter or decision)

Picture it!
If hand contact is control, then a matter out of my hands is a matter I don't have control over.

Example:
I can't do anything about the pay raise you asked for. It's **out of my hands.** The company has a policy of no raises for employees this year.

 get a grip
Maintain or regain control of your emotional state

Picture it!
A grip is a firm hold on something. Getting a grip on anything will control or stabilize it.

Example:
That was a terrible thing to say to your neighbor, John. **Get a grip!**

hit me up for
Ask for—and usually get—a loan or a favor

Picture it!
Hitting is forceful contact. It can convince someone to do something—with an implication, sometimes, of coercion.

Example:
My father-in-law **hit me up for** twenty dollars for some charity he works for.

be a soft touch
Be easily persuaded (often to give money)

Picture it!
Some people must be gripped firmly to be controlled. Others need only to be touched softly and they respond. If it is easy to get money or some other goods from you, then you are a soft touch.

Example:
My uncle Peter **is a soft touch.** All you have to do is ask for a dime and he gives you a dollar.

get out of hand
Become wild, unruly, out of control

Picture it!
Hand here is generic, meaning all hands. If hand contact is control, then *out of hand* means "out of control."

Example:
When the home team was losing the soccer game, things **got out of hand.** There was a lot of screaming, and people were running out of the stadium.

CONTROL IS CONTACT VIA STRINGS

 11 **pull strings**
Use influence to get favors done

Picture it!

A marionette is a kind of puppet, a figure of a person or animal, that has strings attached to its arms and legs. Pulling the strings makes it do what you want.

Example:

My uncle works for the police department. He **pulled some strings** and got my parking ticket revoked, which saved me twenty-five dollars.

12 **string me along**
Make me wait (usually deceiving)

Picture it!

To string me along is to pull me by a string, controlling my movements.

Example:

Donald said he loved Yvonne, but he was just **stringing her along.**

13 **tied to your mother's apron strings**
Unable to make independent decisions, unable to act differently from what is expected

Picture it!

Mothers normally make their children do what is expected. An apron is what a person wears to protect his or her clothes from spills. If you are tied to your mother's apron strings, you are very controlled.

Example:

Herman is so **tied to his mother's apron strings** that he won't even play baseball after school unless he calls his mother to get permission.

 at the end of my rope
At the limit of my patience or endurance

Picture it!
You can give an animal more freedom to act by giving it more rope. Being at the end of your rope means that you have no more to give and must control the situation.

Example:
I'm **at the end of my rope** with one of my students. He never does his homework and he's late to class every day.

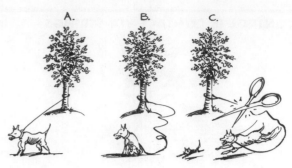

 cut me some slack
Give me a little freedom to do what I want, take it easy on me

Picture it!
The rope in A is taut: it has no slack. The rope in B has a lot of slack. If you cut the rope (C), the dog has unlimited slack, and is not under any control.

Example:
I have a wedding to go to tomorrow, and I have a paper due for Professor Wise, so I think I'll ask him to **cut me some slack**—maybe let me turn the paper in next week.

 rein in
Decrease the scale, intensity, or incidence of something

Picture it!
Reins are straps attached to the mouths of horses and some other animals. Pulling the reins in makes the animal slow down.

Example:
I need to **rein in** how much I spend on traveling in order to save money for health insurance.

Understanding and Using Idioms

Complete the sentences with idioms from the list.

fly off the handle	*gotten out of hand*	*rein in*
out of my hands	*get a grip*	*pin me down*
pulling strings	*carried away*	*up in the air*
at the end of their rope	*hit me up for*	*a soft touch*
cut me some slack	*string men along*	*get ahold of*
tied to his mother's apron strings		

Professor Gold Lectures on Darwin's Dangerous Ideas

Does human psychology really evolve the way that species do? It is not hard to

_____ on that question: my opinion is, absolutely not. But some
　　　　1

researchers, whom we call evolutionary psychologists, think that women have

developed the capacity to _____ so that they will help take care of
　　　　　　　　　　　　　　2

children. These evolutionary psychologists think that this deception is necessary

because men have no basic interest in the process of raising children. If that is

true, I am an evolutionary mistake, for I love taking care of my children. My son is

in college, like you, and he wants to live off campus because he thinks he has been

_____ at home. So he wants a car, and he just _____
　　　　3　　　　　　　　　　　　　　　　　　　　　　　　　　　　　　4

$10,000 to buy one. And I can assure you that I am not _____.
　　　　　　　　　　　　　　　　　　　　　　　　　　　　　5

　　As an editor of the journal *Psychology of Tomorrow,* part of my job is to

_____ ideas that have become too radical. And as your teacher,
　　　　6

I must warn you about ideas that are like universal acid. Universal acid is an acid

that is so strong that it dissolves everything. The problem is that there can be no

container for it. One of these dangerous ideas is that natural selection explains

everything that humans do. Of course, we must not leave the definition of natural

selection _____, so I will define it as the process by which better
　　　　　　　7

adaptations to the environment survive while others die out.

　　I must apologize for giving such an imperfect definition, but I hope you

will _____, as students often say, since I have much to
　　　　　8

accomplish in a very short time. Recently, the concept of natural selection has

_____. It has even been applied to psychology. So you can see
　　　　9

how easy it is to be ————————— with the idea. These authors need to

————————— themselves and be careful about spreading radical ideas.

Consider the evolutionary psychologist idea that all human behaviors are adaptations for survival—even aggression. Should we really believe that aggression, which could lead to our destruction in this nuclear age, was a beneficial adaptation? As a simple example, if you take a wrong turn while you are driving and your passenger starts aggressively complaining and acting completely crazy, should you react aggressively—start a fight, or just tell him to —————————? How is it beneficial to ————————— every time someone does something to annoy us?

You probably have read about the many teenage girls who deliberately injure themselves. We assume that these girls do these things in order to exert some little bit of control over their parents. The girls are, in fact, very troubled. They are —————————. But evolutionary psychologists believe that ————————— this way is due to a basic Darwinian adaptation: the girls are forcing their parents to devote more time and resources to them. So a seemingly bad adaptation is seen as an effective one. An interesting idea, but one that I don't really agree with. Anyway, whether these ideas are accepted or not is —————————. You—the future scientists and psychologists—will be the jury that decides.

Conversation Questions

Pair Work. Ask each other the following questions. If your partner asks for additional information, use your imagination to think of something. If you hear a very interesting response, share it with the class.

1. I'm sorry if you feel like I'm **pinning you down** on a difficult question, but what do you really want to do in life?

2. My sister is **up in the air** about what college to attend next year, and I'm not even sure what kinds of things she should be considering in making that choice. Could you help? What factors should she be taking into consideration?

3. Do you ever **get carried away** when you're talking about some subject? What is it you **get carried away** with?

4. Do you ever **fly off the handle?**

5. I've been lying awake all night worrying about the TOEFL test next week. I can't sleep. I can't eat. My roommate said, **"Get a grip!"** I'm not sure why she/he said that. What do you think?

6. I failed my English test, so I started thinking about dropping out of school, maybe getting a job washing dishes. And my roommate said, **"Get ahold of yourself."** But I wasn't sure what he/she meant. What *did* he/she mean?

7. My English teacher gave me a C for the course and I went back and asked her to reconsider my grade because I tried really hard and my presentation was good, but she said it was **out of her hands** now. Do you think she's telling the truth? I mean, if a teacher really wants to change a grade, she can do it, right? I mean, what if she had made a mistake?

8. Have you ever been in a class or a situation when students really **got out of hand?**

9. Suppose you needed to borrow ten dollars. Do you know anyone who is **a soft touch?**

10. My friend Aaron **hit me up for** twenty dollars, then twenty dollars more and, you know, ten here, ten there, and I gave him the money because he's starting a new jewelry business. He makes rings and other jewelry. So I keep loaning him money. He says we can go into business together, if I want. But I don't know. Do you think he's just **stringing me along?**

11. Do you know anyone who can **pull strings?**

12. Do you know anyone who is **tied to his or her mother's apron strings?**

13. Do you remember any teacher who was **at the end of his or her rope** because of an unruly student? What did he or she do about it?

14. When I talk to my friends, I like to use a lot of slang. But my parents say I should always speak in a more refined manner. Do you think they should **cut me some slack?**

15. Has your country been successful in **reining in** inflation?

Understanding and Speaking

Pair Work. Complete the conversation with the idioms in the list. Read the conversation with a partner, and then switch roles and read it again.

hit you up for	*up in the air*	*rein in*
flew off the handle	*a soft touch*	*get out of hand*
get ahold of yourself	*stringing her along*	

Holden: So, how's your relationship with Barbie going?

Bart: It's kind of ――――――――. As soon as I started talking about
                                    1

my doubts about romantic love she ――――――――. She accused
                                                         2

me of ――――――――. Now I feel like jumping off a bridge or
                    3

something.

Holden: Bart, _____, man. Like, take some deep breaths or
4

something.

Bart: I was thinking about the famous stories of romantic love—Romeo and

Juliet, Tristan and Isolde, Heloise and Abelard, Bonnie and Clyde—

they're all so tragic. These relationships just seem to

_____. I don't want to end up like them.
5

Holden: Yeah, I know, man, because then you'd be dead, man. Maybe you should

_____ this relationship before you get killed
6

or something. And, I mean, if you're not taking Barbie our for pizza,

maybe I could _____ five dollars.
7

Bart: I'm broke, man. Try Desdemona. She's _____.
8

Creative Conversation

Complete the conversation, using the numbered hints. Read the conversation twice with a
partner, changing roles the second time. Do not look at your partner's text. You must remember how your partner filled in the blanks so that you can respond in an appropriate way.

1. some dinner food

2. something easy to make a decision on

3. name some of the things you have to do
   to make pizza, or things you have to buy

4. amount of money needed for pizza

5. something Harry might spend his
   money on, for example, tropical fish

6. something you could put on the dish to
   make it taste better

Harry: Honey, what made you decide on _____ tonight instead of
1

pizza?

Sally: So now you want pizza? Usually I can't **pin you down.**

Harry: Don't **fly off the handle,** hon. I didn't say I wanted pizza. I just wondered

why we're having _____.
1

Sally: This is really crazy. You're always **up in the air** about everything. You

can't even decide _____. I'm **at the end of my rope**
2

waiting for you to make a decision on anything.

Harry: **Cut me some slack,** Sal. Yesterday I had no problems deciding

_____. I'm just cautious. All I want to know is why we
2

can't have pizza.

Sally: Why can't we have pizza? I'll tell you why. I don't have time to

_____. Besides, I don't have enough money to buy the
₃

ingredients.

Harry: You could **hit your mother up for** _____ bucks.
₄

Sally: Last week you were complaining that I was **tied to my mother's apron

strings.** Now you want me to **hit her up for** _____?
₄

If you didn't spend our money on those stupid _____,
₅

we'd have money for pizza. But tonight we're having

_____. You'll have to **rein in** your appetite for
₁

Italian food.

Harry: I guess we're having _____.
₁

Sally: Yup. _____. Sit down and eat the _____.
₁ ₁

Put some _____ on it if you like.
₆

Harry: Hmm. _____ and _____. Not bad. See,
₁ ₆

I made a decision. I'm a decisive guy, deep down. Really.

Sentence Completion

Finish these sentences.

1. I finally **pinned** _____ **down** on his/her opinion about _____

_____.

2. I used to be **up in the air** about _____, but now _____

_____.

3. I was only going to buy _____, but I **got carried away** and

_____.

4. _____ **flew off the handle** when I said that _____

_____.

5. **"Get a grip!"** I said to _____ when he/she _____

_____.

6. You really have to **get ahold of yourself** when _____

_____.

7. _____ said that the decision to _____ was **out of his/her hands,** which made me angry because _____

_____ .

8. A party can **get out of hand** if _____

_____ .

9. _____ is such **a soft touch** that _____

_____ .

10. I **hit** _____ **up for** _____ in order to _____

_____ .

11. If I found out that _____ was **stringing me along,** I would

_____ .

12. You need someone to **pull strings** when _____

_____ .

13. _____ was **tied to his/her mother's apron strings.** For example,

_____ .

14. I remember _____ being **at the end of his/her rope** because

_____ .

15. I tried to get my father to **cut me some slack.** His rules are so strict. I can't even

_____ .

16. _____ should **rein in** his/her appetite for _____

because _____

_____ .

Writing and Speaking

Write six Conversation Questions similar to the ones on pages 98–99, using idioms from this chapter. Then ask and answer these new questions with a partner.

1. _____

_____

2. _____

_____

3. _____

_____

4. _____

_____

5. _____

_____

6. _____

_____

American Art 101

Look at the painting *Sunlight in a Cafeteria* (1958) by Edward Hopper and use five idioms from this chapter to tell what is happening in the painting, or how you feel about the painting, or what one of the people in the painting might say.

Example: This cafeteria scene does not look like one that could get out of hand.

1. _____

_____

2. _____

_____

3. _____

_____

4. _____

_____

5. _____

_____

Rewriting Using Idioms

Rewrite the following piece of art criticism, using idioms from this chapter and preserving the sense of the passage. You will have to do more than simply substitute phrases for the italicized words: sometimes you will have to change the structure of the sentence.

It is hard to *make a precise, unambiguous statement about* what the characters in the cafeteria are thinking. But that is what is so fascinating about Hopper's work. We have a sense that the characters, who look perfectly normal and average on the surface, are struggling to *maintain control of their emotional states,* especially in dealing with their loneliness. We have a sense that the man and the woman here are *decreasing the intensity of* their emotions, as society instructs, and we are silently urging them to give free rein to those emotions.

We feel the man's self-doubt. He seems about to speak to the woman, but he is saying to himself, *"Control your emotions."* The woman, too: notice the turn of her head, as if she were about to speak but can't.

Is city life necessarily like this—the alienation, the lack of communication? The outcome of this encounter is completely *unsettled.* That sadness, and indeterminacy, are part of Hopper's genius.

Presentation

Prepare a short presentation (up to five minutes) to the class on any topic you wish. Use as many of the idioms in this chapter as you feel comfortable with.

Suggested Topics

A famous love story in your country

An idea that some people think is
    universal acid

An example (examples) of pulling strings

Something that you (or other people) need
    to rein in

chapter 9

BASIC METAPHORS
- People Are Food
- People Are Animals

INTRODUCTION There is an old saying in English: "You are what you eat." It is not surprising, then, to find that a basic metaphor in English is *People are food.* The characteristics we associate with food become associated with people. And this association is not limited to idioms. We talk about people being "sweet" or "bitter." Given this very common feature of English, and of many other languages, it is easy to see why many idioms can be understood via this basic metaphor.

Many of us have names that originally belonged to animals: both nicknames like Tiger and surnames like Wolff, Fox, and Bird. There may be no metaphor in English more basic than *People are animals.* Many idioms may be understood via this basic metaphor, as we find many occasions to express the similarity of animal characteristics and human ones.

WARM-UP In your country, do you sometimes call a person a shark, or a lion, or some other animal? If so, what characteristics of that animal can be applied to humans? Share your answers with a group of three or four.

Throughout the world adults tell children stories in order to teach them something. These stories are called fables. In the United States, one famous collection of these is called *Aesop's Fables.* But fables are slightly different in different countries, revealing differences in cultural values. For instance, the fable "The Tortoise and the Hare" ends differently in Japan and in the United States. If you know that fable, tell it. See if the other members of your small group know it and if it ends the same or differently in their countries. If differently, what cultural values are reflected in the different ending?

PEOPLE ARE FOOD

1 chew out
Scold or criticize strongly

Picture it!
If you chew on someone it will hurt, just as strong criticism can hurt.

Example:
When the students were late three days in a row, the teacher **chewed them out.**

 a big cheese

An important person (usually said sarcastically)

Picture it!

Some cheese has a very noticeable smell. A big cheese will be very noticeable. The sarcasm comes from the fact that the smell is sometimes unpleasant.

Example:

If you want a raise in pay, you have to be nice to **the big cheese.**

 the cream of the crop

The best of anything

Picture it!

Cream rises to the top, and the top is associated with the best. And cream is considered the best part of unhomogenized milk.

Example:

Only **the cream of the crop** gets admitted to Harvey College. It is a very selective college.

 a couch potato

An inactive person, one who sits on the couch all day watching TV

Picture it!

A potato grows underground, unseen, and is inactive. These characteristics can be applied to a person who sits on a couch all day watching TV.

Example:

My friend David is such **a couch potato.** He's gained a hundred pounds in two years.

PEOPLE ARE ANIMALS

 5 to bitch / a bitch
To complain / a woman who complains a lot, a very unpleasant woman

Picture it!
A bitch is a female dog. A dog that is barking loudly at you can seem to be complaining. In English, most comparisons of people to dogs are negative.

Example:
I wish my uncle would stop **bitching** about bad drivers while we are having dinner. It's so unpleasant. (**Note:** *Bitch is considered vulgar and is generally used in anger or irritation.*)

6 weasel out of
Avoid doing something you should do as a responsible person

Picture it!
A weasel is a foxlike animal that is not easily caught and tends to avoid detection.

Example:
My little sister **weaseled out of** doing the dishes again, so I had to do them.

7 wolf down
Eat something quickly, with poor manners

Picture it!
We imagine that wolves eat their prey—other animals—quickly, and they obviously do not have human manners.

Example:
I had just ten minutes for lunch before my next class, so I **wolfed down** three pieces of pizza and just made it on time.

8 **be a turkey**
Be a jerk, be a fool

Picture it!
A turkey is a very unintelligent animal.

Example:
You**'re** such **a turkey!** All you needed to do for the final exam was to review basic math and you didn't do it.

9 **chicken out / be (a) chicken**
Act in a cowardly manner / be a coward

Picture it!
A chicken is one of the least brave animals.

Example:
I was going to dive off the five-meter board, but when I got up there I **chickened out.**

10 **ahead of the pack**
Leading, in a superior position compared to the majority

Picture it!
Wolves and some other animals roam in groups called *packs*. Any animal that is ahead of the pack leads it and will be the first to realize the pack's objective.

Example:
In computer programming, you have to keep learning new languages if you want to stay **ahead of the pack.**

11 black sheep

Outcast, group member that the rest of the group rejects

Picture it!

Black sheep are less common and less valuable than white sheep. Also, black sheep were once considered to be marked by the devil.

Example:

My whole family are doctors and lawyers, except my brother Pablo, the painter. He's the **black sheep** of the family.

12 be bullish (on)

Be enthusiastic about the prospects of something (usually used in the area of finance, for example, the stock market)

Picture it!

A bull is an aggressive animal. A person who is enthusiastic about a stock or something pursues it aggressively.

Example:

I **am bullish on** computer makers. I think these companies are going to have a very profitable year.

13 be bearish (on)

Be unenthusiastic about the prospects of (usually used in the area of finance, for example, the stock market)

Picture it!

A bear hibernates all winter. Because it is so inactive in that season, it cannot do anything enthusiastically.

Example:

Most financial analysts **are bearish on** gold. They think the price will decrease another ten percent this year.

14 clam up

Refuse to talk

Picture it!

A clam is a shellfish. When it closes its shell, it cannot be opened easily. The closed shell resembles a tightly closed mouth.

Example:

The child **clammed up** when she was asked who broke the vase.

15 monkey with
Try to get something to work better, in a trial-and-error manner

Picture it!
A monkey can manipulate objects to get what it wants, but it does so without much thinking, in a trial-and-error way.

Example:
I've been **monkeying with** my VCR for two hours, and I still can't get it to record.

16 monkey business
Silly, mischievous, or dishonest conduct

Picture it!
Monkeys can be very clever in imitating human conduct. They can escape from their cages (which we see as mischievous).

Example:
Johnny, stop that **monkey business** and get to work!

Understanding and Using Idioms

Complete the sentences with idioms from the list.

monkey business	chewing out	turkeys
ahead of the pack	big cheese	bitched
couch potatoes	bullish	wolfed down
weasel out of	monkey with	chickened out
clammed up	bearish	black sheep
the cream of the crop		

Professor Goodman Lectures on Nietzsche and Truth

As you know, many of Friedrich Nietzsche's contemporaries did not accept his

ideas. He was a ———————— among philosophers. "I come like a lion,"
                              1

he wrote. And to continue the animal metaphor, he never ———————— of
                                                                    2

a dispute.

He thought that philosophers who believed in opposites like good and evil or truth and falsity were misguided ——————3——————. Nietzsche might even have rudely called them that to their face—he was very blunt. He enjoyed ——————4—————— these philosophers, especially when they talked about truth. Nietzsche was ——————5—————— on truth. And I think that time has proven that Nietzsche was on the right track. Truth is often irrelevant and seldom comprehensive.

Contemporary philosophers who are ——————6—————— on truth might ask you to consider the word *white.* If I point to it and say, "Is it true that this is white?" you would answer, "Yes." But suppose I asked this question of an illiterate person. He might truthfully say, "No, it's black," looking at the color of the ink. Should we dismiss such a person because he is not ——————7—————— intellectually?

If you are still not convinced, let me try another example. Suppose Fred says, "2 and 2 is 5," and I say, "2 and 2 is a bluebird." Neither statement is true, but Fred's is much more relevant. To him, you might say, "You're wrong." To me, you might say, "What kind of ——————8—————— is this?"

Finally, I want you to consider the case of my friend Mary Tricias, who saw a little cupcake in a bakery and said, "I want enough for fifty people, just like that." The bakery later delivered a ten-pound cake, and Mary was upset. Excuse me for saying so, but normally Mary would have ——————9—————— about it. When the baker said that the cake was a true representation of her order, she didn't know what to say. She just ——————10——————. In any case, her guests ——————11—————— the cake that afternoon. Let me add that I, unfortunately, was not one of them. I had to give a presentation at a conference attended by all the ——————12—————— philosophers. And when you are the guest of honor, there is no way to ——————13—————— the commitment.

Now, since our time is up and this was our last class, I have a surprise for you— a ten-pound cake. I had to ——————14—————— the recipe, since it was originally for a one-pound cake, but I think you'll like the result. And if you are concerned about your grades and want to get ——————15——————, I suggest you read Nietzsche tonight and not turn into ——————16——————.

And *that* is true.

Conversation Questions

Pair Work. Ask each other the following questions. If your partner asks for additional information, use your imagination to think of something. If you hear a very interesting response, share it with the class.

1. Does **the cream of the crop** of young athletes get special treatment in your country? If so, describe the treatment. If not, should they?

2. Do you know anyone who is **a big cheese?** What is he or she like?

3. Do you know any **couch potatoes?** What programs do they watch? Why do you think they became **couch potatoes?**

4. In the United States, some college students will **bitch** about their grades directly to the teacher's face. Does this happen in your country?

5. Have you ever been **chewed out** in public?

6. When you were a kid, did you have chores you didn't like to do? And did you ever **weasel out of** doing them?

7. Do you ever **wolf down** meals? If so, why? And what is your personal record for **wolfing** something **down?** I mean, how fast and how much?

8. In your country, if a student had the opportunity to look at the final exam ahead of time and didn't do it, would he or she **be** considered **a turkey** or a person of integrity?

9. Suppose there are ten candidates running for president. What is the best way for one of them to get **ahead of the pack?**

10. Kids often dare each other to do things, and when a kid won't do something, he or she is called **chicken.** Has this happened to you? If not to you, then to someone else? Describe the incident.

11. Is there **a black sheep** in your family?

12. Are you **bullish on** the economy of your country at the beginning of the twenty-first century?

13. My financial advisor is **bearish on** technology stocks for the next few years. Do you think I should sell all my technology stocks?

14. My friend **clams up** every time the subject of fathers comes up. Why do you think she **clams up** like that?

15. My wife's car sometimes doesn't start right away, and sometimes it slows down for no reason. I know I can fix it by **monkeying with** the carburetor, but she wants to take it to a garage where they'll charge a hundred dollars for a ten-minute job. Do you think I should just **monkey with** it and not tell her?

16. In recent years American male politicians have gotten into trouble because of **monkey business** with women they are not married to. Does this kind of **monkey business** get as much publicity in your country? How is it viewed?

Understanding, Speaking, and Writing

Write a conversation between two students, Holden and Ellen. For each speech, read the description of what the student wants to say, then transform that information into one or more sentences, replacing each italicized phrase with an idiom. You must write out the entire speech, not just the idiom. Read the conversation with a partner, each partner taking one role. Then switch roles and read the conversation a second time. (Note: To *assent* is to say words like *yeah, yes, OK, hmm, all right,* or *right.* To *suggest* is to use a phrase like *Let's,* or *Why not,* or *I suggest.*)

Thelma suggests going to McDonald's and *eating a burger very quickly,* and Ellen can tell her about her favorite philosopher.

Thelma: _____

_____

Ellen asks if Thelma really wants to know. He is not one of the *important persons* of the philosophy world.

Ellen: _____

_____

Thelma assents.

Thelma: _____

_____

It is Woody Allen.

Ellen: _____

_____

Thelma replies that he is not a philosopher. He is a comedian.

Thelma: _____

_____

He is both a philosopher and a *very important* comedian. He said something like, "Can we actually know the universe? It's hard enough finding your way around Chinatown."

Ellen: _____

_____

Thelma agrees that, among comedians, he is *the best.* He was invited to be a member of some club once, and he declined, saying that he would never want to be a member of any club that wanted him.

Thelma: _____

_____

That reminds Ellen of one of her professors, who is always *complaining* about the international students at Harvey College speaking their own languages. He stopped a group of students and *strongly criticized them to their faces*. He said, "Stop speaking Japanese. You are in America now. Speak Spanish, for goodness' sake!" And the students *became silent*.

Ellen: _____

_____

The students probably didn't get it. They didn't understand that in Miami you hear more Spanish than English.

Thelma: _____

_____

Creative Conversation

Complete the conversation, using the numbered hints. Read the conversation twice with a partner, changing roles the second time. Do not look at your partner's text. You must remember how your partner filled in the blanks so that you can respond in an appropriate way. In this conversation, you will be a reporter who is going to interview the artist Andy Warhol, before his death in 1987.

1. interesting city
2. number of hours it would take
3. period of time
4. something cheap (a couch)
5. product that has an expiration date on it

6. some state or city
7. something else you could do in bed
8. amount of time
9. animal

You: Mr. Warhol, don't you think that _____ is more inter-
$_1$
esting than New York?

Warhol: Yes, but I'm **bullish on** New York. In New York it takes _____
$_2$
to go downtown, and another _____ to go back uptown,
$_2$
so you don't have time to be interesting. And the people in New York are

so famous. I was talking to Yoko Ono, who was constantly complaining

because her three cats haven't talked since her husband, John Lennon,

died. And I said mine **clammed up** for _____ once, but I
$_3$
wouldn't **bitch** about it.

You: Is it true you chewed out Bob Dylan for trading the Elvis painting you

gave him for a _____?
$_4$

Warhol: Absolutely not. Paintings should have an expiration date on them, like

_____. And every month you put everything expired in
          5

a box and drop it in _____.
                              6

You: And who is your favorite philosopher?

Warhol: Proust. He said something like, "How much better it would be if we
never went out of our rooms." I'm a **couch potato,** really. All you need
is a bed. Everything is more glamorous in bed. You can do everything
in bed—paint, **monkey with** your latest sculpture, eat, peel potatoes,
or _____.
                7

You: You've been compared to Picasso. Do you think that's a fair comparison?

Warhol: I've been compared to all the **big cheeses.** When Picasso died, I read he
had made four thousand masterpieces in his life. And I thought, "Gee,
I can do that in _____."
                        8

You: Do you believe in God?

Warhol: I believe in reincarnation. I want to be reincarnated as a big ring on
Pauline de Rothschild's finger. And you?

You: I don't believe in any of that spiritual **monkey business.** I think reincarnation is a way of **weaseling out of** death. But if I could be reincarnated,
I'd come back as a _____.
                             9

Sentence Completion

Finish these sentences.

1. Only **the cream of the crop** of actors _____

   _____.

2. This person I know, Mr./Mrs. _____, thinks he/she is **a big
   cheese** in _____ , but in reality he/she _____

   _____.

3. I wouldn't mind being **a couch potato** for a while because I could _____

   _____.

4. My friend _____ is always **bitching** about _____

   _____.

5. My boss **chewed me out** because _____
_____.

6. My friend _____ always finds a way to **weasel out of** paying
for _____ when we _____
_____.

7. The last time I **wolfed down** _____ was when _____
_____.

8. _____ **is** such **a turkey.** I mean, last week he/she _____
_____.

9. In my home city, _____, if you want to see someone like
_____ in concert, you should get there **ahead of the pack,**
because _____, so you have to _____
_____.

10. My friend was going to _____, but he/she **chickened out**
because _____
_____.

11. Woody used to get invited to all the big parties, but then he became **a black
sheep** when he _____,
_____ and now he never gets invited.

12. I'm **bullish on** the teaching profession. I think _____
_____.

13. I'm **bearish on** the _____ profession. I think _____
_____.

14. _____ will **clam up** if you ask him/her _____
_____.

15. I made the mistake of letting _____ **monkey with** my
_____ when it wasn't working, and the result was that _____
_____.

16. Before he left for work, my father said to my brother and me (we were nine
and ten), "No more **monkey business,** OK?" He was referring to the fact that
the day before, we _____
_____.

Writing and Speaking

Write six Conversation Questions similar to the ones on page 112, using idioms from this chapter. Then ask and answer these new questions with a partner.

1. _____
   _____

2. _____
   _____

3. _____
   _____

4. _____
   _____

5. _____
   _____

6. _____
   _____

American Art 101

Look at the painting *The Studio* (1969) by Philip Guston and use five idioms from this chapter to tell what is happening in the painting, or how you feel about it, or what the hooded figure in the painting might say.

Example: Many art critics are really bullish on Guston's semiabstract art.

1. _____
   _____

2. _____
   _____

3. _____
   _____

4. _____
   _____

5. _____
   _____

Rewriting Using Idioms

Rewrite the following piece of art criticism, using idioms from this chapter and preserving the sense of the passage. You will have to do more than simply substitute phrases for the italicized words: sometimes you will have to change the structure of the sentence.

Philip Guston was an abstract and a post-abstractionist artist. He was a gifted painter, but he could also draw extremely well. He won a drawing contest when he was a student. He was articulate, intelligent, and handsome. He even worked in Hollywood when he was a teenager. He could have become an actor, but he was not interested in Hollywood's *dishonesty and immorality*. Instead, he went to Italy to study the masters. He *was enthusiastic about* artists like Piero della Francesca. Guston thought that Piero was *the best* of the Renaissance artists.

Guston worked feverishly in his studio. This painting is a self-portrait of the artist painting a self-portrait. Guston smoked constantly, and only put down a cigarette to *eat a sandwich quickly*.

Notice, too, that the artist is depicted as a Ku Klux Klansman,* suggesting, to my mind, that the artist must be subversive. But we never see the Klansman's mouth. The artist has *gone silent*, suggesting that we have to interpret the world ourselves. Perhaps Guston is also suggesting that, instead of trying to get *into a superior position* financially, we should look within ourselves and see what evil tendencies we all have.

* *Ku Klux Klan: a very controversial organization whose members believe, among other things, that white people are superior to other races.*

Presentation

Prepare a short presentation (up to five minutes) to the class on any topic you wish. Use as many of the idioms in this chapter as you feel comfortable with.

Suggested Topics

Racism in your country or in the United States

Your favorite abstract artist

Reincarnation

A great comedian

A great philosopher

chapter 10

BASIC METAPHOR	Part A: The Beginning of the Journey
• Life Is a Journey	The End of the Journey

INTRODUCTION In every language, life is understood and explained as a journey. There are so many points in common. Just as every journey has a beginning, middle, and end, so does life. Logically, we use journey metaphors to communicate what is happening in our lives. Some of these are very obvious (for example, "I *stepped into* a new job," which means "I *began* a new job"). Other metaphors are harder to understand, and we tend to call these *idioms*.

If *life is a journey*, then any project you have in life is also a journey—it has a beginning, a middle, and an end.

WARM-UP Knowing that life is a journey and that the various activities in our lives are also journeys, work in small groups (three or four) to figure out the meanings of the following metaphorical descriptions. Your teacher can verify whether your guesses are correct.

1. The boss just gave me my *walking papers.*
2. We have invested $100,000 and we cannot *turn back* now.
3. They got divorced last week, but it wasn't surprising, because their marriage had been *on the rocks* for years.
4. Peace negotiations have *stalled*, and many observers think that they won't *go* anywhere even if they *get started* again.

THE BEGINNING OF THE JOURNEY

1 get your feet wet
Start on a new job or venture

Picture it!
In order to swim, you usually start by putting your feet in the water.

Example:
I really didn't want to go to college, but once I **got my feet wet** I loved it.

 get it off the ground
Get it started

Picture it!
When a plane is off the ground, it is on its way to its destination.

Example:
As soon as we get the loan from the bank, we can **get** this business **off the ground.**

 **start out on the wrong foot**
Start badly, making a mistake

Picture it!
If you start a dance with the wrong foot, you may step on your partner's foot.

Example:
Didi, you **started out on the wrong foot** when you showed up late for work on your first day.

 miss the boat
Fail to take advantage of an opportunity

Picture it!
The boat represents the journey that you are not embarking on.

Example:
I could have gone to law school, but I decided to have fun instead. Now, I regret it. I guess I really **missed the boat.**

 pave the way for
Make progress or development easier

Picture it!
To pave is to put asphalt or cement on a dirt road.

Example:
In the sixteenth century, Tycho Brahe carefully wrote down the positions of the stars. This **paved the way** for Keppler's discovery of the orbits of the planets.

 be on the verge of
Be about to do something

Picture it!
A verge is a border. If you are at the verge of a road, you are about to cross it; in other words, you are about to act.

Example:
I **am on the verge of** quitting my job. If I have to work another twelve-hour day, I'll quit.

▲ **give someone the green light**
Give someone permission to start something

Picture it!
The green light of a traffic signal means *go*. If you are stopped at a red light and it turns green, you have permission to start moving.

Example:
The company is about to market its new weight-loss drug. Company officials are just waiting for the drug regulatory agency to **give them the green light.**

THE END OF THE JOURNEY

 8 go downhill
Deteriorate, function poorly

Picture it!
If the journey of life is seen as going over a hill, then the start is going up, and going down means going to the end, or death. Going to the end is deterioration.

Example:
Our basketball team was doing well until Michael retired. Now it's **going downhill.** We've won twenty-five games and lost thirty.

9 pass away
Die

Picture it!
Since 1300, it has been common to speak of dying as "passing away" or "passing on." We pass along the journey of life. Then we pass away from existence.

Example:
My grandmother **passed away** last week. She was 91 and active until her very last day.

 10 end of the line/road
The end of some development or of one's life

Picture it!
A railroad track is often referred to as a *line.* At the end, the journey is over.

Example:
This is **the end of the line** for me, my friends. Tomorrow I retire from this business.

11 it's all downhill from here

Easy from this point

Picture it!

Another way to look at *downhill* is from the point of view of riding a bicycle. It is hard work to go **up** the hill, but it is easy to go **down.**

Example:

It has taken us five years to get this business going, but now we can relax. **It's all downhill from here.**

Understanding and Using Idioms

Complete the sentences with idioms from the list.

starting out on the wrong foot	*on the verge of*	*passed away*
giving you the green light	*paves the way*	*going downhill*
all downhill from here	*end of the road*	*missed the boat*
get your feet wet	*get off the ground*	

President Murphy Welcomes the Class of 2001 to Harvey College

Good morning. I see a few vacant seats, so I guess that some students have already

_____, unless they are from overseas, in which case their absence
₁

is understandable. But these students won't miss anything crucial; classes will not

_____ for two more days. And at Harvey College we have what
₂

is called a "shopping period," which means that during the first week you can

attend classes without officially registering for them. This gives you a chance

to _____.
₃

Now I notice that some students are just arriving, and look like they have been

out dancing till 3:00 A.M. These students are _____. If they are not
₄

careful they will be _____ from day one. I'm sure this is not the
₅

impression your parents wanted you to make. This kind of behavior only

_____ for failure.
         6

As you know, college is harder than high school. So don't get too worried if you

get a C on your first exam. Just remember that one poor grade does not mean it is

the _____ for your academic career.
       7

Well, I will make this short because I want to give you a chance to relax and get

some rest. You have a tough week coming. It is not _____. I urge
               8

you to familiarize yourselves with the pleasant little town of Sleepy Hollow, but

that doesn't mean I'm _____ to party all night. I wish you luck. You
           9

are _____ a great four years. Now I think we should have a
      10

moment of silence for our previous president, who _____ just two
                  11

months ago.

Conversation Questions

Pair Work. Ask each other the following questions. If your partner asks for additional information, use your imagination to think of something. If you hear a very interesting response, share it with the class.

1. Do you ever have the feeling that you're **missing the boat** in some way? If so, how?

2. I have a date with Peggy Sue next Saturday, but I'm afraid her father won't like me because I wear an earring. Is there anything I can do to avoid **starting out on the wrong foot** with him?

3. Have you taken a lot of English courses, or are you just **getting your feet wet**?

4. Can you think of a famous actor, actress, or sports star who is **at the end of the road**?

5. Tell me about some restaurant, school, or city that, in your opinion, has **gone downhill.**

6. If you could be reincarnated as an animal after you **pass away**, which animal would you like to be? Why?

7. If my parents **give me the green light**, I'm going to get a tattoo. Do you think I'll regret it?

8. I **was on the verge of** asking my girlfriend to marry me, but my parents wouldn't **give me the green light**, so I didn't. Do you think I should just go ahead and do it?

9. I want to start a school for teaching English, but I don't know how to **get it off the ground**. Do you have any suggestions?

Understanding, Speaking, and Writing

Write a conversation between two students, Holden and Bart. For each speech, read the description of what the student wants to say, then transform that information into one or more sentences, replacing each italicized phrase with an idiom. You must write out the entire speech, not just the idiom. Read the conversation with a partner, each partner taking one role. Then switch roles and read the conversation a second time. (Note: To *assent emphatically* is to use an expression like *sure, of course,* or *certainly.* To *suggest* is to use a phrase like *Let's,* or *Why not,* or *I suggest.*)

Bart asks what Holden thought about President Murphy's speech.

Bart: _____

Holden was falling asleep. He asks what Bart thought.

Holden: _____

Bart doesn't know what to think. He missed the first part. He was one of those guys the president said *started badly.* Bart's father says he has been *deteriorating* since he hit thirteen. His father doesn't have much faith in him.

Bart: _____

_____

_____

Holden does. Bart *is about to become* famous as a party animal. By the time he leaves Harvey College, he will be famous for his parties—but only if he starts now. Holden suggests having one tonight.

Holden: _____

_____

_____

Bart asks if they have time to *get it started.*

Bart: _____

_____

Holden assents emphatically. They might not get A's on their tests, but they will throw excellent parties.

Holden: _____

_____

This might be *the end of the development* of their academic careers.

Bart: _____

_____

Holden's father says that socializing *makes success in business easier.* You have to make friends if you want to influence people. In other words, Holden's father is *giving them permission.* Besides, no one ever flunks out of Harvey. Once you get in, *it's easy.*

Holden: _____

_____

_____

_____

Creative Conversation

Complete the conversation, using the numbered hints. Read the conversation twice with a partner, changing roles the second time. Do not look at your partner's text. You must remember how your partner filled in the blanks so that you can respond in an appropriate way.

1. occupation
2. number
3. clothing suitable for the occupation
4. reason for having reservations about that career

Thelma: I'm worried about my new job. I've never been a

_____ before.
　　　　1

Louise: Well, it's time to **get your feet wet.** By the time you've finished

_____ days here, you'll know all about being
　　　　2

a _____ .
　　1

Thelma: You're experienced at this. What do you think I should wear my

first day?

Louise: A good _____ should wear
　　　　　　1

_____ her first day on the job. But you
　　　3

don't want to **start out on the wrong foot,** so wear a very good

_____ .
　　3

Thelma: I'm so nervous. I'm **on the verge of** giving up this idea. I don't

want to **miss the boat,** but I have reservations about being a

_____ because _____ .
　　1　　　　　　　　　　　　4

Louise: Relax, Thelma. After a week you'll know everything you need to

know, and **it will all be downhill from there.**

Sentence Completion

Finish these sentences.

1. This is your first day in the United States, so you need to **get your feet wet.**
   Why don't we _____

   _____?

2. Honey, all of our friends are having kids. I have the feeling that we're **missing the boat.** Maybe we should _____

   _____.

3. "Look, Virginia, I'm sorry we **started out on the wrong foot.** I know I
   shouldn't have taken you to Burger King on our first date. Next time we'll

   _____."

4. A good education **paves the way** for _____

   _____.

5. I want to start a _____. And in order to **get this thing off the ground,** I need to _____

   _____.

6. My friend **was on the verge of** becoming a good _____
   but unfortunately _____

   _____.

7. Just **give me the green light** and I'll _____

   _____.

8. Diego is a great soccer player. But I think he's at **the end of the road** because

   _____.

9. Service at restaurants in _____ (name of city) has really
   gone downhill. For instance, the last time I ate there, _____

   _____.

10. In some countries it is a struggle to get into college, but once you do, **it's all downhill from there.** I mean _____

    _____.

11. When the dictator **passed away,** _____

    _____.

Writing and Speaking

Write six Conversation Questions similar to the ones on page 124, using idioms from this chapter. Then ask and answer these new questions with a partner.

1. _____

_____

2. _____

_____

3. _____

_____

4. _____

_____

5. _____

_____

6. _____

_____

_____

Presentation

Prepare a short presentation (up to five minutes) to the class on any topic you wish. Use as many of the idioms in this chapter as you feel comfortable with.

> Suggested Topics
>
> What to expect your first day at
> _____ (name of a
> college or university)
>
> What to expect your first day in high
> school
>
> What to expect your first year of marriage
>
> What to expect your first day on the job at
> _____ (name
> of company)
>
> My experience with employment agencies

chapter 11

INTRODUCTION   All the idioms in this unit deal with the middle of the journey, which metaphorically is the middle of a project or action.

WARM-UP   Let's look at how ordinary language is structured with *journey* metaphors, particularly the middle of the journey. If life is a journey, then any activity in your life is also a journey. In small groups (three or four), discuss the meanings of the following sentences that use journey metaphors to describe a relationship. Discuss also how the sentences are metaphorical; in other words, what is compared to what?

1. We've been *down that road* before.
2. We are just *spinning our wheels.*
3. We've *gotten off the track.*
4. I don't think this relationship *is going* anywhere.

THE MIDDLE OF THE JOURNEY

1 get cold feet
Retreat from something you started, usually from fear

2 take it in stride
Not let something disturb you

Picture it!
We know that to get your feet wet means to get started at something. But if the water is too cold, you will get out rather than continue to swim.

Picture it!
To stride is to walk or run at a regular speed, covering the same distance with each step. When a horse jumps over an obstacle as if it were not there, the horse takes it in stride.

Example:
I was going to invest $20,000 in the stock market. Then I **got cold feet** and decided to leave the money in the bank. Even though I only get 2 percent interest, there is no risk.

Example:
You failed the math test, Albert, but just **take it in stride.** You'll still pass the course.

3 on the fast track
In a position in which fast advancement is assured

Picture it!
One track may be faster than another.

Example:
Yesterday, my law firm hired a woman who just graduated from law school, and they're paying her $90,000. And you should see her office—it's got a view of the Charles River. She's definitely **on the fast track.**

4 social climber
A person who tries hard to improve her or his status in society, often by being artificially nice to people of high class (This is viewed as negative in the United States because there are more important things in life than one's position in society.)

Picture it!
Social success is pictured as a ladder.

Example:
Ralph is just a **social climber.** He invites all those rich people to his parties and laughs at their stupid jokes that aren't funny.

5 up and running
Functioning normally

Picture it!
To be up and running is to be in the middle of the journey.

Example:
I couldn't use the computers at school last night because we had a power failure. But this morning the electricity was back on and all the systems were **up and running.**

 drag your feet
Deliberately slow down a process

Picture it!
You can slow down your bicycle, for example, by dragging your feet. This applies to any process.

Example:
Cindy could get her Ph.D. this year, but she's **dragging her feet** because she likes studying more than working.

 follow in someone's footsteps
Follow someone's example or take someone's guidance

Picture it!
A person's decisions on the journey of life are like footprints, which we can follow by making similar decisions.

Example:
Joan's father was a lawyer, then a senator. Joan is a lawyer, too, and it appears she will **follow in her father's footsteps** and enter politics.

 go through
Experience, suffer

Picture it!
The event is like a tunnel. When you go through the tunnel, you are on the other side of the event.

Example:
I **went through** a terrible divorce last year. I hope you never have to **go through** anything like that.

 burn bridges
Commit oneself to an irreversible course

Picture it!
The person crossed the bridge, burned it, and now cannot go back.

Example:
Since you told Roseann that her cooking was terrible, she is upset with you. I'm afraid you've **burned your bridges.** She'll never invite you again.

10 **be on board**
Be part of a company, enterprise, or group project

Picture it!
To be on board means to be on a ship, where everyone is together and has the common goal of reaching a destination.

Example:
Thanks for hiring me here as your new soccer coach. I'm glad to **be on board.**

 don't rock the boat
Don't destabilize the situation

Picture it!
If you rock the boat (make it go back and forth), you might make it turn over, which is dangerous and would probably make the other passengers unhappy.

Example:
I hate doing business with that company, but I don't want to **rock the boat** since I'm new on the job. So I won't say anything.

12 **in the wake of**
Following, or as a consequence of, some event

13 **be in the same boat**
Be in a similar situation

Picture it!
The wake of a boat is the waves it makes when it is moving fast. The wake always follows, and is caused by, the boat.

Picture it!
The boat is a metaphor for *situation*. Both people here are in a dangerous situation.

Example:
Housing and food shortages became critical **in the wake of** the hurricane.

Example:
If I don't pass the final exam in chemistry, I'll fail the course. My roommate is **in the same boat** because she also failed the midterm exam.

Understanding and Using Idioms

Complete the sentences with idioms from the list.

in the same boat	*in the wake of*	*on board*
drag your feet	*social climber*	*gone through*
take it in stride	*on the fast track*	*get cold feet*
burn their bridges	*rocked the boat*	*up and running*
follow in their footsteps		

Professor Davies Lectures on Time Travel

In the history of science, there have always been revolutionaries—Galileo and Darwin, for example. These original thinkers often got into trouble because they

_____.
1

And new ideas have always been considered dangerous. These thinkers had to

_____ with previous scientific thought and set out on a new path.
2

Since I am one of the few physicists who take the idea of time travel seriously, I

guess I am _____ with the revolutionary thinkers.
3

Our common-sense feeling about time is that it flows. That is our first mistake.

Time does not move. We move in it. All of time—past and future—exists at any moment. To travel in time, forwards or backwards, means to move to a parallel universe. Some physicists, probably like you, follow my idea of time to some extent, but they _____4_____ when I introduce the idea of parallel universes, of which there are an infinite number.

And some people have a problem with the idea of changing the past. But in reality, changing the past is no different from changing the future, which we do all the time. This may be hard for you to accept, but I hope you will try to

_____5_____.

Suppose that people in the future build a time machine and get it _____6_____. Suppose they travel back to visit us. Can we expect to _____7_____? Not at all, because our future is not theirs. They will have come from a parallel universe. However, if their society has _____8_____ some disaster, they could warn us of it. We might want to change the way we are doing things if we know about the problems they faced _____9_____ such a disaster.

People who don't believe in the possibility of time travel mention some version of the following problem. Suppose a historian travels back to the year 1600 in England. At this time Shakespeare is _____10_____ of literature. Our traveler shows Shakespeare scenes from *Hamlet* (which hasn't been written yet), and Shakespeare likes them so much he writes them into the play he calls *Hamlet.*

Who actually wrote it? Perhaps someone actually *did* travel back in time with all of Shakespeare's plays and gave them to a young actor named William Shakespeare, who then claimed to have written them! Remember, Shakespeare was considered by some to be a _____11_____ in the theatrical world.

The truth is that Shakespeare wrote the plays—but Shakespeare in a different universe, one of an infinite number of versions of that person. Some of you will resist believing that. You will _____12_____, but I'm going to pull you along this fantastic journey into the idea of time travel. This course will explain that idea thoroughly. I am glad to have you _____13_____.

Conversation Questions

Pair Work. Ask each other the following questions. If your partner asks for additional information, use your imagination to think of something. If you hear a very interesting response, share it with the class.

1. Suppose you were the head of the English department at a big university and you could hire a famous writer to work there. Is there anyone you would especially like to have **on board?** Anyone you definitely would not want to have **on board?**

2. We are supposed to go to an ESL (English as a second language) convention in California. They just had a strong earthquake there. **In the wake of** this, do you think I should go? Why or why not?

3. Most of my English teachers just have their classes do grammar exercises. Now this new teacher wants everyone to speak. Do you think it's a good idea for her to keep **rocking the boat?**

4. I need a better job and a higher salary. Do you know anyone **in the same boat?**

5. Have you ever **gone through** an earthquake? If so, what was it like?

6. My girlfriend moved out of her parents' house and they got angry. Do you think she has **burned her bridges** by moving out?

7. Do you know a **social climber?** If so, describe him or her.

8. At what time in the morning do you have to be **up and running?**

9. I can't figure out why my sister is **dragging her feet** buying a new car. Hers is twelve years old and is falling apart. Why do you think she is **dragging her feet?**

10. My neighbor was going to adopt a child. She was so excited about it. Then it seemed she **got cold feet.** And she hasn't talked about it for months. Can you think of any reason why she might have **gotten cold feet?**

Understanding and Speaking

Pair Work. Complete the conversation with the idioms in the list. Read the conversation with a partner, and then switch roles and read it again.

in the same boat	*in the wake of*	*on board*
social climber	*took it in stride*	*on the fast track*
follow in the footsteps	*rock the boat*	

Holden: Do you get the impression that President Murphy wants to

_____ of Ronald Reagan and be president of the
   1

United States?

Bart: You know, that's really perceptive. In fact, Murphy has always been

_____, and he won't stop at being president of Harvey
   2

College. You know, I think Murphy and Reagan were both in the navy.

Maybe that's why Murphy always welcomes everyone

"_____."

3

Holden: Right, but the difference between Reagan and Murphy is that Reagan

was never a _____. I think Murphy cares too much

4

about making friends in high places.

Bart: I think he cares too much about making money. Did you hear about the

million dollars he spent remodeling the president's house?

Holden: No.

Bart: Yeah. Big scandal. But he was so calm. He just _____.

5

I don't understand why the university trustees don't fire him.

Holden: Because they're all _____. He gets them higher salaries

6

and does them favors too. So why would they _____?

7

Bart: You sure are cynical for a freshman.

Holden: Hey, _____ so many political scandals it's hard not to

8

be cynical. It's our generation.

Creative Conversation

Complete the conversation, using the numbered hints. Read the conversation twice with a partner, changing roles the second time. Do not look at your partner's text. You must remember how your partner filled in the blanks so that you can respond in an appropriate way.

1. a reason he can't hear her (the radio is on)

2. describe her bad cooking or some awful dish that she makes

3. amount of time (30 minutes, 4 days)

4. amount of time they've been married (10 years)

5. kind of car (Chevy)

6. kind of store

7. product you would buy at the store in number 6

Martha: George, I think we should get a divorce. You never listen to me.

George: What's that, honey? I can't hear you. _____.

1

Martha: I said we should **burn our bridges,** get a divorce.

George: I can't hear you, hon. Did you say something about a fire?

Martha: Divorce! I want a divorce!

George: Ow! You don't have to shout. You said the same thing last year at this time, then you **got cold feet.** I think you're just upset **in the wake of** our

visit to your mother's house. All I said was that _____.

                                                         2

Martha: If you stopped complaining for _____, that would

                                              3

be a milestone in our marriage.

George: _____ is about all the time I want to stay married to

                              3

you. You've been **rocking the boat** ever since we got married

_____ ago.

                                              4

Martha: Well, I'm glad you're **taking this in stride.** And I'll be glad to be rid

of you. Your idea of being **on the fast track** is driving a '57

_____ to the _____ to

                              5   6

buy _____.

                      7

Sentence Completion

Finish these sentences.

1. President Murphy was going to suggest that _____, but

   he **got cold feet** because _____

   _____.

2. Dale, I'm sorry that Roy _____,

   but you have to **take it in stride.**

3. Diana is such a **social climber.** Did you see her at Jack's party? She _____

   _____.

4. If telephone service isn't **up and running** by tomorrow, _____

   _____.

5. If you want to be **on the fast track,** you should _____

   _____.

6. I wouldn't mind **following in** _____'s **footsteps.** I mean,

   _____.

7. The reason that _____ is **dragging his feet** on

   _____ is that _____

   _____.

8. I hope we don't **go through** another winter like the last one. The snow was so

deep that _____

_____ .

9. Jane will never get another job with the nuclear power industry. She really

burned her bridges behind her when she told the newspapers _____

_____ .

10. **In the wake of** _____'s successful reelection campaign, we

will probably see _____

_____ .

11. We had eighteen inches of snow yesterday. I called my mother in Buffalo and

she said they **were in the same boat.** In fact, _____

_____ .

12. The whole family decided to watch the football game on TV. Then Bart, as

usual, had to **rock the boat.** He said _____

_____ .

13. "My most important bit of news is that I have appointed a new minister of

_____," said the president. "We're glad to have her **on**

board because _____

_____ ."

Writing and Speaking

Write six Conversation Questions similar to the ones on page 135, using idioms from this chapter. Then ask and answer these new questions with a partner.

1. _____

_____

2. _____

_____

3. _____

_____

4. _____

_____

5. _____

_____

6. _____

_____

Presentation

Prepare a short presentation (up to five minutes) to the class on any topic you wish. Use as many of the idioms in this chapter as you feel comfortable with.

Suggested Topics

Teachers' salaries

Salaries of _____

A big strike

Why you think labor unions are good/bad

The college you went to or go to

chapter 12

Part C: More about Journeys

INTRODUCTION   This basic metaphor *Life is a journey* generates three additional metaphors. These three metaphors follow logically from the premise that life is a journey. We call these *derived metaphors*. The first derived metaphor is that *Life is a race.* You can easily understand how this metaphor derives from the idea that life is a journey. A journey can take many forms. A race is one of these forms. So the connection is clear. We have goals in life, which are like the finish line in a race.

The second derived metaphor is *Problems are constraints on a traveler.* A constraint is something that holds you back, something that holds back progress. If motion on a journey is constrained, the traveler is stalled or stopped. Therefore, problems are seen as constraints.

The third derived metaphor is *Problems are barriers on a journey.* A barrier is something that stops or impedes. Problems in life are like barriers in a journey.

WARM-UP   Write three goals in your life. Do you feel like you are in a race to achieve them? Why or why not? Share these goals and your feelings with a group of three or four.

LIFE IS A RACE

 run for (office)
   Try to get elected

Picture it!
The goal of an election is to win, just as the goal of a race is to win.

Example:
If the governor of New York **runs for** president, it will be a close race.

 fall behind
Not stay on schedule for completing a project

Picture it!
Just as you can fall behind in a race, you can fall behind in achieving any of the goals in your life.

Example:
I **fell behind** on my term paper because I had four tests to study for.

 start from scratch
Start from the beginning again (often after a failure)

Picture it!
In a race, *scratch* is the starting line, which originates from scratching a line in the ground.

Example:
I spent an hour trying to program my VCR, but I failed. Now I have to **start from scratch.**

 jump the gun
Start before you are supposed to

Picture it!
A gun is often fired to signal the start of a race. To jump the gun is to start before the gun is fired.

Example:
We were supposed to hand in our proposals on Friday, but Johnny Cheathem **jumped the gun** and handed his in on Thursday.

 (a lot) riding on it
(A lot) depending on the outcome of some event

Picture it!
When you bet money on a horse, you put money on it, metaphorically. The outcome of the race, therefore, is very important, for the money is riding on it. In the same way, any project you have can have a lot riding on it.

Example:
I hope you pass the TOEFL exam. There's **a lot riding on it.**

PROBLEMS ARE CONSTRAINTS ON A TRAVELER

 in a rut
Doing the same monotonous, boring thing

Picture it!
A rut is a depression in a dirt road made by wheels following the same path.

Example:
I'm **in a rut.** All I do is correct papers. I need a change. Maybe a vacation. I can't think anymore.

 in a tight spot
In a difficult situation

Picture it!
A tight spot is a place in which it is hard to move. Your motion is constrained, so you can't easily do what you want to do.

Example:
Virginia, I'm **in a tight spot.** I know we were supposed to meet at eight o'clock, but I promised Bill I'd give him a ride home. So, would you mind if I'm a half hour late?

8 **cooped up**
Confined in a small space, therefore with little to do for fun

Picture it!
A coop is a place where chickens are kept. It is usually small and crowded.

Example:
I'm tired of being **cooped up** in here. I wish the snow would melt and spring would come so I could get out once in a while.

 between a rock and a hard place
In a dilemma, between two equally undesirable choices

Picture it!
This idiom is an example of what we call *dry humor*. It is funny because a rock *is* a hard place—there is no difference. Such a situation is also called a *no-win* situation.

Example:
I'm stuck **between a rock and a hard place.** If I live with my parents after college, I won't have any privacy. But if I move out, I won't have any money.

PROBLEMS ARE BARRIERS ON A JOURNEY

10 **run into problems**
Encounter problems

Picture it!
Problems are barriers you may encounter on the journey to your destination.

Example:
I was going to marry Julia, but I **ran into problems.** You see, I found out she was already married to Bruce.

11 **hit twenty (thirty, forty, etc.)**
Reach the age of twenty (thirty, forty, etc.)

Picture it!
It is often a psychological shock to reach a certain age because we want to be young forever. So, reaching that age is like hitting a wall.

Example:
I know your birthday is tomorrow and you're anxious about **hitting thirty,** but thirty is not so bad. Wait till you **hit forty!**

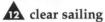 **clear sailing**
Absence of problems

go through with something
Complete a project (usually after hesitating)

Picture it!

If the water in front of your boat is clear, there are no problems in front of you. Also, a clear sky is one that does not present problems (storms).

Picture it!

One often pauses before an obstacle to reconsider one's options. Going through is continuing the journey.

Example:

My husband and I went through some stormy weather. I mean, we had some serious problems, but since we saw a marriage counselor it has been **clear sailing.**

Example:

I've been thinking about resigning. I don't like my job. But I don't know if I'll **go through with it.** I'm not sure I could find another job very soon.

 come through for me
Overcome an obstacle and do something that I need

Picture it!

A person who comes through does something that would be difficult, overcoming an obstacle on the journey of life.

Example:

Do you remember when I broke my leg and couldn't do anything? Every day you made my meals and helped me get dressed. You really **came through for me.**

Understanding and Using Idioms

Complete the sentences with idioms from the list.

between a rock and a hard
   place
came through for
ran into problems
a lot riding on

start from scratch
hit twenty
went through with
in a tight spot
jumped the gun

fall behind
in a rut
clear sailing
cooped up
run for

Professor Millikan Lectures on Physics

I want to take you on a journey into the extraordinary world of subatomic
particles. And the most fascinating physicist in that area is Richard Feynman. Feynman was already doing advanced physics before he _____. When-
ever he was _____, unable to find a new way to think about physics
problems, he would picture the problem in terms of an everyday event. For
example, when he _____ thinking about the spin of an electron, he
pictured an ordinary sprinkler he used to water the
lawn. We know what happens when water shoots out—
the sprinkler spins around. But would it spin in the same direction, or the opposite
direction, or not spin at all if water were sucked in?

It looks simple, but there was _____ the outcome, in terms of
theory. And in another thought-experiment, Feynman wondered why
it is that when we look in a mirror the reflection is reversed from left
to right. Your right hand becomes your left hand. Why isn't it
reversed top to bottom, so that your head and feet are reversed?

Here again, comparing the problem of an electron's motion to an ordinary event
_____ Feynman. Finally, there is the famous puzzle of *Schrodinger's
cat:* to make a long story short, the cat is in a box and is neither dead nor alive till it
is observed. The physicist/observer is _____—if he opens the box
he may, by observing, kill the cat. If he doesn't, the cat will starve to death.

Some of you may remember the disaster of the space shuttle *Challenger,* which
blew up in 1986, killing seven people. Prior to that time, America's space shuttle
program had enjoyed _____. Feynman appeared on television,

explaining what had gone wrong to millions of viewers. Again he used an ordinary example to illustrate it. He dropped a piece of a small but crucial part of the shuttle, a kind of ring made of rubber, into a glass of ice water. Then he showed how it became less elastic. NASA (National Aeronautics and Space Agency) officials had _____8_____, sending the shuttle up before the air was warm enough to safely do so. Some scientists thought it was dangerous to do so, knowing that there was a 14 percent chance of failure, but the mission heads _____9_____ it anyway. Some NASA officials may have been worried that their program would _____10_____ if they delayed launching the shuttle. Because of previous delays, they might have felt that they were _____11_____, pressured to get the shuttle up on schedule. But the disaster set America's space program back. Engineers had to _____12_____ to design new rings that would be safe in colder weather. Because of television, Feynman became famous enough to _____13_____ political office, but he had no desire to.

There are many famous stories about Feynman, like when he was interviewed by a psychiatrist for military service in 1946. The psychiatrist asked him if he felt _____14_____ in large rooms. And Feynman replied that that was the way he felt at the moment, and that he was in the biggest room he'd ever been in. And when he was asked if he heard voices in his head—a sure sign of craziness—he replied that he did so all the time. He had conversations with Einstein, Newton, even God.

Feynman never did military service. And if you're still wondering about the sprinkler—it doesn't move at all, as Feynman correctly predicted.

Conversation Questions

Pair Work. Ask each other the following questions. If your partner asks for additional information, use your imagination to think of something. If you hear a very interesting response, share it with the class.

1. Would you like to **run for office** some day? Why or why not? If yes, which office?

2. What do you recommend to a student who habitually **falls behind** in his or her studies?

3. What would you recommend to a tenant who regularly **falls behind** in his or her rent payments?

4. I'm supposed to get married in September, just before school starts. But I am inclined to **jump the gun** by a couple of months, just elope, no big wedding. Am I crazy?

5. My computer died during a storm and my whole twenty-page term paper was lost. Should I **start from scratch** or just buy a paper like half the class does?

6. I'm **in a tight spot** because I lost money betting on some football games. Do you think I should ask my boss to help me out, or should I ask my in-laws, who are rich?

7. I know a teaching assistant in math who is in love with one of her students. On the one hand, she wants to keep it a secret. On the other hand, she wants to spend Christmas with his family in England. Do you think she is **between a rock and a hard place?**

8. Have you ever felt **cooped up?** If so, explain.

9. My friend says she is **in a rut** after three years of marriage and wants to know if this is normal. What should I tell her? And what should I tell her to do to get out of **the rut?**

10. Do you think you will get married (divorced) before you **hit thirty?**

11. My friend says that having a baby is rough for the parents, but after the kid hits three it's **clear sailing.** Do you agree?

12. I gave some kid I don't know a dollar to buy me a soda and I told him he could keep the change. Do you think he'll **come through for me** or run off with the money?

13. I planned to buy a car, but I just got married and we're going to live very close to my work. Do you think I should **go through with** the car purchase?

14. If you moved to a country where you didn't speak the native language, where do you imagine you would first **run into problems?**

Understanding, Speaking, and Writing

Write a conversation between the mathematician Euclid and the physicist Albert Einstein. For each speech, read the description of what the student wants to say, then transform that information into one or more sentences, replacing each italicized phrase with an idiom. You must write out the entire speech, not just the idiom. Read the conversation with a partner, each partner taking one role. Then switch roles and read the conversation a second time. (Note: *Disbelief expressions* are phrases like *Come on! No way! Give me a break! Approval expressions* are phrases like *Great! Fine,* or *Good.* To *suggest* is to use a phrase like *Let's,* or *Why not,* or *I suggest.*)

Everything up here has been *marked by the absence of problems.* But Euclid feels that he is *doing the same monotonous thing.*

Euclid: _____

_____

Einstein tells Euclid that he has been *inside the small space of* his pyramid too long. Einstein suggests going over to Galileo's place and having a look through his telescope. He'll show Euclid how gravity slows down light.

Einstein: _____

_____

_____

Euclid is afraid that they might *encounter difficulties* tonight. It looks like rain.

Euclid: _____

_____

Disbelief expression. The last time it rained up here was when Euclid *reached* 1,000. Einstein asks if they should take Euclid's camels or his.

Einstein: _____

_____

Euclid prefers to take Einstein's, if Einstein doesn't mind. Euclid is in *a difficult situation.* He told Plato he could borrow his any time, and though Plato rarely comes out of his cave, Euclid would feel bad if Plato came by and there weren't any camels.

Euclid: _____

_____

_____

Approval expression. On the way Einstein will tell Euclid about his relativity theory. Euclid will love it. There is *so much depending on the outcome of it*—mankind's whole conception of the universe.

Einstein: _____

_____

_____

Approval expression. Euclid knew that Einstein would *overcome obstacles for him.*

Euclid: _____

_____

Creative Conversation

Complete the conversation, using the numbered hints. Read the conversation twice with a partner, changing roles the second time. Do not look at your partner's text. You must remember how your partner filled in the blanks so that you can respond in an appropriate way.

1. number
2. edible liquid (ketchup)
3. a reasonable but not large annual salary
4. Sally's age
5. number (the number in number 1, plus 2)
6. number
7. family member (sister)
8. a nice outdoor place (the Grand Canyon, Lake Geneva)
9. subject of study
10. a fish (ask teacher for a list if you don't know any)
11. something essential (or inessential, if you wish!—for example, a toothbrush)

Sally: I'm tired of being **cooped up** all day with _____ kids
1

while you're having long lunches with the boys.

Harry: Hey, Sally. I don't need this today. I spilled _____ on
2

the boss today at lunch and I'm afraid he might fire me.

Sally: Good! Why don't you throw the _____ in his face, then
2

quit and get a job that pays more than _____ a year?
3

Harry: I think you're going through some kind of crisis, Sally. I mean, ever since

you **hit** _____ you've been acting strange. How can
4

you expect me to quit my job when I've got _____
5

mouths to feed? We go through _____ quarts of milk
6

a day. I'm going to have to buy a cow. And it would have to be a big cow

to **come through for us.** You know, maybe we should just drop the kids at

your _____'s and go to _____.
7   8

Sally: You know I would love to, Harry. I love _____. But
8

I'm taking this course in _____, and I'm afraid I'd
9

fall behind.

Harry: Why don't you come? Forget _____. We can forget
9

all our problems and **start from scratch.**

Sally: I feel like I'm **between a rock and a hard place.** I have a test on Monday.

And there is **a lot riding on it.**

Harry: Honey, it's just a stupid grade. Wouldn't you rather eat fresh

_____ cooked on an open fire under a starry sky in
       10

_____ ?
       8

Sally: OK. Let me pack some clothes.

Harry: Clothes? Who needs clothes? All you need is _____ .
                                                                    11

That's all.

Sally: When did you get so romantic?

Harry: The thought of fresh air and delicious, fresh _____
                                                                  10

does it to me. Let's go.

Sentence Completion

Finish these sentences.

1. If _____ ,

   you have to **start from scratch.**

2. If _____ had not **run for** president of

   _____ , then _____ .

3. If a candidate **falls behind** in an election, it is probable that _____

   _____ .

4. There is not much **riding on** _____

   _____ .

5. The good thing about **jumping the gun** and exchanging Christmas presents the

   day before Christmas is _____

   _____ .

6. I'm **in a tight spot,** Holden. Could I copy your _____

   homework? I don't have time to do it because _____

   _____ .

7. The president was **between a rock and a hard place.** If he sent troops abroad to

   restore peace, the American people might _____ ; but if he

   didn't send them, the local people would _____ .

8. I hate being **cooped up** in _____

_____.

9. If you get **into a rut** at your job, _____

_____.

10. You will **run into problems** if _____

_____.

11. When I **hit forty,** _____

_____.

12. After _____,

it will be **clear sailing.**

13. Sally threatened to divorce Harry, but I don't think she'll **go through with it**

because _____

_____.

14. I was so happy when dad **came through for me** that time I was in Rome and

_____.

Writing and Speaking

Write six Conversation Questions similar to the ones on pages 146–147, using idioms from this chapter. Then ask and answer these new questions with a partner

1. _____

_____

2. _____

_____

3. _____

_____

4. _____

_____

5. _____

_____

6. _____

_____

Presentation

Prepare a short presentation (up to five minutes) to the class on any topic you wish. Use as many of the idioms in this chapter as you feel comfortable with.

Suggested Topics

How psychiatry is viewed in your country

Should there be mandatory military
    service for all young people—both male
    and female?

Military service in your country

An election in your country

chapter 13

INTRODUCTION There are many different types of card games, and they are the source of many metaphors. In this chapter, we will learn idioms that are metaphors derived from card games. Once you see how the idiom is used in a card game, you can see how it applies, metaphorically, to other areas of life. Because card games are competitive, the idioms that come from them are often used in competitive situations.

WARM-UP If you know a game of cards that is very easy to teach, bring a deck of cards to class and show your group of three or four how to play it. Try to learn the necessary card vocabulary, and ask your classmates for help if there is a term you do not know.

CARDS

 1 to ace (a test)
To get an A (an excellent grade)

2 deal with
Be occupied with, act in a certain way toward

Picture it!
In a standard deck of fifty-two playing cards, the highest card is the ace. Receiving the highest grade is like getting the highest card.

Picture it!
To deal cards is to distribute them to the players. When you deal with people, you are, in a sense, distributing your attitude toward them.

Example:
I'm doing so badly in this course. I'll have **to ace** the final exam just to pass.

Example:
Bill refuses to **deal** with Sam because Sam cheated him last year.

 make a deal
Offer or arrange an agreement

Picture it!
When you deal someone a card, you are offering that card. The person who picks it up accepts the deal—the arrangement.

Example:
Let's **make a deal.** I'll do the cooking, and you pay the rent.

 Big deal!
So what? Who cares?

Picture it!
When used alone, the two words *big deal* mean the opposite of what you would think. You picture a great hand, perhaps four aces (in a hand of five cards). So this idiom can be mildly sarcastic.

Example:
So the United States soccer team beat Mexico. **Big deal!** They'll never win the World Cup.

 wheel and deal / wheeler-dealer
Act in one's own interest, aggressively and often unscrupulously / a person who acts in such a way

Picture it!
If you wheel and deal, you play both roulette and cards, which makes you a big bettor, with lots of money. Self-interest and unscrupulousness are associated with gambling.

Example:
André is a **wheeler-dealer** in computer sales. He **wheels and deals** all over the world, selling every kind of computer there is.

 a bum deal
Bad transaction, unfair treatment

Picture it!

Bum means "unfair" or "bad." If you receive bad cards, you have received a bum deal.

Example:

When the Boston Red Sox traded the great baseball player Babe Ruth to the New York Yankees for just a few thousand dollars, that was **a bum deal** for the Sox.

 play your cards right
Make good use of your resources, use good strategy

Picture it!

If you have been dealt good cards, you still have to play the right card at the right time, according to a strategy.

Example:

If you **play your cards right,** you could end up marrying that rich pianist.

8 **have something up your sleeve (have a card up your sleeve)**
Have a secret plan or resource

Picture it!

One way to win at cards is to have a good card hidden in the sleeve of your shirt.

Example:

Skip bet me a hundred dollars that he could beat me in a boat race. But his boat is so old that I am afraid he **has something up his sleeve.** Maybe that old boat has a jet engine in it.

 lay your cards on the table
Reveal your plans or position honestly

Picture it!
In a poker game, you keep your cards hidden while you are betting. At some point, it is necessary to reveal what cards you have—by laying them down on the table.

Example:
You should **lay your cards on the table** with Ralph. Tell him exactly how you feel about him.

 the luck of the draw
Pure chance, whether good or bad

Picture it!
In some card games you draw (take) a card from the deck. It is a matter of luck whether the card is good or bad.

Example:
I bought a twenty-five-cent cigar and it was terrific, but that's **the luck of the draw.** A lot of twenty-five-cent cigars are bad.

 the deck stacked against you
Many difficulties face you unfairly

Picture it!
To stack a deck of cards is to arrange it so that the draw is not by luck. If I put a queen first and an ace second, and you draw first and I draw second, I stack the deck against you.

Example:
I went to a school in Texas where almost everyone but me was bilingual, so in my Spanish class **the deck was stacked against me.**

 bluff / call your bluff
Pretend to be in a stronger position than you actually are / expose the fact that you are bluffing

Picture it!
You can win a game of poker even when you have a bad hand (bad cards) by betting a lot of money. This may cause the other players to think you have very good cards, so they will not match your bet, which means you win automatically. If someone thinks you actually have bad cards despite your high bet, she or he will not fold but will match your bet. This is called *calling your bluff.*

Example:
My parents said that if I come home at midnight again they are going to throw me out. But I think they're just **bluffing.** And I'm going to stay out until 1:00 A.M. tonight and **call their bluff.**

 hold all the cards
Be in a winning position

Picture it!
If you hold all the cards, or even all the desirable cards, your opponents cannot possibly win.

Example:
Our labor union has asked for a raise in hourly pay, but the company **is holding all the cards.** They can easily replace us because we have no specific skills.

to fold
To go out of business, to admit defeat

Picture it!
To fold your cards means to put them in a pile face down on the table. This means you are dropping out of the game because you don't think you can win.

Example:
Originally, the union was not going to accept the company's offer, but eventually they **folded.**

Understanding and Using Idioms

Complete the sentences with idioms from the list.

lay my cards on the table	wheeler-dealers	ace
up my sleeve	call our bluff	fold
the luck of the draw	holding all the cards	bluffing
play your cards right	making a deal	bum deal
the deck stacked against you	deal with	

Professor Eugene Nicks Speaks on Genetic Engineering

If you could create perfect human beings, would you do it? Some scientists—
geneticists—think they can. They are the _____ of genetic
1
engineering. But now, suppose a lot of *perfect* humans were born. When it comes to
succeeding at anything, you would have _____ all the time because
2
you couldn't compete with them. You would say to your parents, "Mom and Dad,
this life is a _____. All these genetically engineered kids
3
_____ all the tests. And when it comes time to find a job, they
4
are _____."
5

No longer could a parent say to a son or daughter, "If you _____,
6
you will end up with a good life." Those who have been genetically engineered
would be smarter, better-looking, more athletic, and healthier. Even life span would
not be _____. These guys are genetically engineered to live 130 years.
7

Recently, we uncovered a secret project that was an attempt to create this master
race. Some years ago, one of the participating scientists told me about it, but I
thought he was just _____. He said, "Well, if you think so, why
8
don't you come to our secret laboratory and _____?" Then he said,
9
"I am going to _____: we need your expertise and we are willing to
10
do almost anything to get it." They were aware of my poor financial situation, and
they pressured me. They were convinced that I would _____, but
11
that would have been _____ with the devil. And since I am talking
12
to you now, I obviously didn't make it. I had nothing _____ but
13
integrity. Sometimes, when you _____ materialistic companies,
14
that's all it takes.

Conversation Questions

Pair Work. Ask each other the following questions. If your partner asks for additional information, use your imagination to think of something. If you hear an interesting response, share it with the class.

1. In what subject would you be most likely to **ace** a test?

2. I told my roommate that I **aced** the English test and he said, **"Big deal!"** Why do you think he said that?

3. Do you know anyone who might be called a **wheeler-dealer?** What does she or he do?

4. Is **the deck stacked against** a foreign student?

5. If you **play your cards right,** do you think you can get a college degree?

6. If you became a **wheeler-dealer,** what is the most likely field you would **wheel and deal** in?

7. I bought a new Ford two weeks ago and everything went wrong with it. Do you think that's just **the luck of the draw,** or does it have something to do with the way I drive?

8. Suppose your boss asked you to lie to an investigator and he said **the stakes were really high,** that the future of the company depended on it. Would you do it?

9. If the phone company told you that you could have free long-distance calls for a week, would you suspect them of **having something up their sleeve?**

10. Do you know of a store or business that **folded?** Why did it **fold?**

11. What will happen if the nations of our planet don't get together and **make a deal** on fishing quotas—I mean, limit the amount of fish that can be caught?

12. My father wants me to go to Boston University but I want to go to Brandeis University. Is he **holding all the cards,** just because he is going to pay for it? Or do you think I might be able to do what I want?

13. The cable TV company is offering cable TV for fifty dollars a month. I don't really know much about the rates. Do you think that's **a bum deal** or a good deal?

14. If someone called you and said he had put a bomb in your school, would you **call his bluff** and go to school?

Understanding, Speaking, and Writing

Write a conversation between Harry and Sally. For each speech, read the description of what the student wants to say, then transform that information into one or more sentences, replacing each italicized phrase with an idiom. You must write out the entire speech, not just the idiom. Read the conversation with a partner, each partner taking one role. Then switch roles and read the conversation a second time. (Note: To *assent* is to say words like *yeah, yes, OK, hmm, all right,* or *right.* To *exclaim* about something is simply to say the words forcefully; in print, you would write them with an exclamation point (!). To *suggest* is to use a phrase like *Let's,* or *Why not,* or *I suggest.*)

Harry wants to *reveal his plans honestly.* It is time for them to have kids.

Harry: _____

_____

It is not that Sally is opposed to it, but she doesn't know if Harry is ready to *be occupied with* a child. But supposing they *arrange an agreement,* how many would Harry want?

Sally: _____

_____

_____

If they have seven, plus Sally and Harry, they can field a whole baseball team.

Harry: _____

_____

Sally exclaims about seven kids. That is *unfair treatment* for any woman. She will spend a large part of the next twenty years pregnant.

Sally: _____

_____

_____

So what? The first six months are pretty normal.

Harry: _____

That is easy for Harry to say.

Sally: _____

Harry assents and suggests that they not argue. He suggests having two kids.

Harry: _____

_____

Sally is still not sure. A child born today *faces many unfair difficulties.* With all the pollution in the environment there is a significant chance of birth defects. Sally means, having a normal child is *pure chance.* And how are they going to afford kids? Unless Harry *has a secret plan,* they can't afford kids.

Sally: _____

_____

_____

_____

_____

If Harry *uses good strategy*, he will get a promotion next month. At least that is what his boss said. And Harry hopes he was not *pretending to tell the truth,* just to get him to work harder.

Harry: _____

_____

_____

Creative Conversation

Complete the conversation, using the numbered hints. Read the conversation twice with a partner, changing roles the second time. Do not look at your partner's text. You must remember how your partner filled in the blanks so that you can respond in an appropriate way.

1. names of a couple who are not happy (Harry and Sally)

2. number (the bigger the number, the smaller the probability)

3. man's name

4. astrological sign (Aries, Taurus, Gemini, Cancer, Leo, Virgo, Libra, Scorpio, Sagittarius, Capricorn, Aquarius, Pisces)

5. astrological sign, different from number 4

6. where you might find true love

7. something to do when you are alone (movies)

8. adjective describing the person (good)

Thelma: Look at all the relationships around you. It's so depressing. I don't want to end up like _____ (1). And it's just **the luck of the draw**—how your partner will turn out in the long run. There is a one in _____ (2) chance that he'll be a good one.

Ellen: One in _____ (2) is optimistic, if you ask me. Maybe you should leave _____ (3). He is a _____ (4), and you are a _____ (5). So **the deck is stacked against you.**

Thelma: I tried to tell _____ (3) that I was leaving him, but he said I was just **bluffing.** And he was right. I went back to him.

Ellen: Men **hold all the cards** in a relationship. That's **a bum deal** for women.

Thelma: Maybe I am just an optimist. I keep thinking that you might find true love _____ (6), and if you **play your cards right,** you might find it. And if you don't—**big deal!** There's always _____ (7).

Ellen: Well, I hope you don't think I've been keeping this **up my sleeve,** but

I've found someone who is _____.
                                                   8

Thelma: This *is* a surprise. I can't wait to meet this guy.

Sentence Completion
Finish these sentences.

1. I think I'll **ace** the _____ test because _____

   _____.

2. I don't like **dealing with** _____ because _____

   _____.

3. I said to _____, "Let's **make a deal:** you _____

   and I'll _____

   _____."

4. You can't ski? **Big deal!** _____

   _____.

5. _____ thinks he's a **wheeler-dealer.** Every day he _____

   _____.

6. I think it was **a bum deal** that _____

   _____.

7. My friend makes only $_____ a year, but she thinks that if

   she **plays her cards right** _____

   _____.

8. On my last birthday I suspected that my father **had something up his sleeve.**

   Here's what happened: _____

   _____.

9. I'm going to **lay my cards on the table** when I see the boss today. I'm going to

   say, _____

   _____.

10. It was just **the luck of the draw** that _____

_____ .

11. I think that **the deck will be stacked against me** if I _____

_____ .

12. _____ is **holding all the cards** in its negotiation with

_____ .

13. The company that made _____ **folded** because _____

_____ .

14. The governor of _____ said that _____

_____ , but I am sure he was **bluffing.**

15. My five-year-old son said that _____ , but I **called his**

bluff, and he _____

_____ .

Writing and Speaking

Write six Conversation Questions similar to the ones on page 159, using idioms from this chapter. Then ask and answer these new questions with a partner.

1. _____

_____

2. _____

_____

3. _____

_____

4. _____

_____

5. _____

_____

6. _____

_____

Presentation

Prepare a short presentation (up to five minutes) to the class on any topic you wish. Use as many of the idioms in this chapter as you feel comfortable with.

Suggested Topics

A card game in your country

Your family vacation

Your opinion about genetic engineering

Should cloning of humans be legal?

chapter 14

BASIC METAPHOR	Part B: Baseball, Football,
• Life Is a Game	Pool

INTRODUCTION The idioms in this chapter come from baseball, football, and pool. Baseball is popular only in certain parts of the world, so the game can seem mysterious to people who have never seen it played. The illustrations will help you to understand the game better and to be able to use the idioms in different contexts.

The peculiarly American game of football is not widely played outside of the United States (Canada and Australia have their versions), but here again the illustrations and explanations will enable you to understand what is going on.

Pool is a form of billiards, played on a table with six pockets. You hit a white ball (the cue ball) with a long stick (a cue stick), which in turn knocks other balls into the pockets, scoring points.

WARM-UP If you understand baseball or American football, and if your group of three or four has some questions about these sports, try to answer the questions and explain the sports. Or you can try to explain how pool is played. Learn whatever vocabulary you can, and ask your group members for help with words you do not know.

BASEBALL

 right off the bat
Instantly

Picture it!
When you hit a baseball with a bat, in most cases the ball instantly bounces off the bat at high speed.

Example:
I met her on Monday, and we became friends **right off the bat.** Now we spend most of our free time together.

 2 go to bat for
Support someone or someone's cause

 3 be a hit
Be a success, be popular

Picture it!
Each baseball player has a turn at bat, trying to hit the ball. A team may substitute a good hitter for a weak hitter: the good hitter goes to bat for the weaker one.

Picture it!
A batter in baseball gets a hit by hitting the ball into the field without the ball being caught and getting to first base before the ball does. This is success for a batter.

Example:
I wanted a raise, and my boss really **went to bat for me.** She told the president of the company that I was a great worker.

Example:
You **were a hit** at the party last night. Everyone wanted to dance with you.

 4 have clout (with)
Have power, influence

Picture it!
To clout means "to hit very hard." A clout is a very powerful hit.

Example:
My boss got me a terrific raise. She **has lots of clout with** the president.

5 **touch base (with someone)**
Make contact (with someone), before taking the next step

Picture it!
The runner must come in contact with first base before advancing to second or third.

Example:
Let's **touch base** before our meeting with the boss. You can call me at home if you want.

6 **hit it off (with someone)**
Get along very well

Picture it!
If you hit the ball off the bat you succeed.

Example:
Dave Brubeck, the great jazz pianist, **hit it off** so well with a girl he met at college that he proposed marriage to her on their first date, and she accepted.

7 **play hardball**
Negotiate toughly, act aggressively

Picture it!
You can play baseball with either a hardball or a softball. You can get hurt more easily playing hardball, which is what most professional teams play.

Example:
The union wants to **play hardball.** They have rejected all our company's offers, which were pretty substantial.

FOOTBALL

8 **kick off (something)**

Start (something—often a group activity)

Picture it!
To start a football game, one team kicks the ball off to the other team.

Example:
This is Bubba Bean at radio station WTGF, and we are about to **kick off** an hour of your favorite country music, with no interruptions.

9 **go for it**

Try to accomplish it, choose it

Picture it!
Let's say you have advanced the football eight yards in three tries, and you need two more yards. You have two options: (1) kick the ball far down field, giving it to the other team; or (2) *go for* the remaining two yards.

Example:
I really shouldn't have any ice cream, especially after two pieces of pie, but I like it so much I think I'll **go for it,** even though I'll gain weight.

POOL

10 **call the shots**

Make the decisions, be in charge

Picture it!
In pool, you have to call your shot, that is, announce which ball you intend to hit into which pocket. You get credit only for balls that go into pockets you have called.

Example:
If I were you, I would not invite Aunt Agnes. She complains about everything. But, hey, it's your party. You're **calling the shots.**

lose your touch
Lose your ability to do something very well

Picture it!
In pool, you need to hit the cue ball with great precision, that is, at the correct angle and with the correct force. This is your *touch*. You can have a *magic touch* or you can *lose your touch*.

Example:
I was stopped for speeding again yesterday, and this time I couldn't talk the police officer out of giving me a ticket. I guess I'm **losing my touch.**

the breaks
Luck

Picture it!
To start a game of pool, fifteen balls are arranged in a triangle, and a player hits the cue ball at them. When the balls scatter, this is the *break*. If one or more balls go into the pockets, this is a good break, and you are lucky. If you are unlucky, well, *those are the breaks.*

Example:
My cousin Vinny spent fifty dollars on lottery tickets this week and he didn't win anything. Well, **those are the breaks.**
(**Note: *Those are the breaks* is an expression of consolation for bad luck.)**

break even
Have your losses equal your gains

Picture it!
In the variation of pool called "8-ball," you have to sink all the balls that have stripes or all the balls that have a solid color ⚫ . When you break, if you sink one striped ball *and* one solid-color ball, you have **broken even.** *Even* here means "fair" or "same."

Example:
We paid $200,000 for our house five years ago. Now we're going to sell it, but the market is poor. We'll probably just **break even.** I mean, we will probably get the same amount we paid for it.

▲14 a long shot
An event of low probability

Picture it!

For most pool players, long shots are harder to make than close ones.

Example:

Your goal is to win an Olympic gold medal? Well, that's **a long shot,** but go for it.

▲15 not by a long shot
Not even close to being possible

Picture it!

A long shot has a small probability of going in. *Not by a long shot*, then, means "not even by a small probability."

Example:

There is no way Nellie is going to win the Kentucky Derby. **Not by a long shot.**

(**Note:** *This idiom is normally used by itself, not as part of a sentence.*)

▲16 Give me a break!
a. Give me a chance or special consideration.
b. I don't believe it!

Picture it!

a. If you *break*, you are in a special position because you are starting and have a chance to get ahead.

b. (ironic) Suppose your opponent breaks, and ten of the fifteen balls go in! This is unbelievable.

Examples:

a. Mom, I'm sorry I got all B's this semester. **Give me a break,** will you? I'm not a genius.

b. You got an A in math!? **Give me a break!** You got a D last semester.

Understanding and Using Idioms

Complete the sentences with idioms from the list.

go to bat for me	*hit it off*	*kick off*
right off the bat	*be a hit*	*clout*
played hardball	*not by a long shot*	*go for it*

Professor Castenon Lectures on Twentieth-Century *Sorcery**

Let me _____ this series of lectures with the story of how I met
1

the great sorcerer Don Juan Matsos twenty years ago in Mexico. I was working

on my Ph.D. in anthropology, studying plants used for healing. I seemed to

_____ with this old Indian who invited me to stay with him,
2

_____. But he was not *just* an old Indian—_____.
3   4

He was a sorcerer. I didn't want to stay with him, but something made me decide

to _____. I think that, in the back of my mind, I knew that I could
5

write a book that would _____. And also that if I
6

_____ with the publisher, I could get an advance of $10,000. But as
7

a young Ph.D. who had never written a book, I knew I didn't have much

_____ with publishers. And my teachers didn't want to look
8

unprofessional or foolish, so they would not _____.
9

Continue reading Professor Castenon's lecture, and complete the sentences with idioms
from the list.

those are the breaks	*break even*	*touch base*
a long shot	*give me a break*	*called the shots*
losing your touch		

I expected him to cook up frogs and snakes and make drinks that make people

fall in love. But what I encountered was a practical philosopher who believed that

there were different worlds, different realities, and that we could enter these by

intent, if we had enough energy. Don Juan lent me his energy to take me to other

worlds by dreaming-awake. I asked if I would be able to do it myself and he said

it was _____. I had to change my life first. I had to change all
10

my old routines. It was hard, and I didn't like it, but if you want to be a

sorcerer, _____.
11

* *Sorcery: witchcraft, dealing with the supernatural.*

Up to then, the only sorcery ability I had was knowing if people liked their coffee black or with cream. I could always guess. I said to Don Juan, "Black, for you."

"Nope. With cream," he said, laughing. "I guess you're _____ ."
12

Then I said, "Don Juan, some things in the material world never change. For example, if I pour cream in your coffee it will dissolve, and your coffee will never be black again."

Then as I watched, his coffee got darker! And finally the cream came together, reversing the dissolving process. I couldn't believe my eyes. "_____ !"
13
I shouted.

"Did you think you _____ ?" he said. "The cream decides, not you!"
14
I was speechless, well, almost speechless.

"That hasn't happened once in a million years," I said.

Don Juan laughed. "When you engage in sorcery, don't expect the usual probabilities. I could toss a coin twenty times and it could come up *heads* every time. Things do not _____ in the sorcerer's world."
15

I knew then that this was not going to be the last of my surprises. But I ran from the scene. I had to _____ with some normal friends before getting
16
more involved with the impossible world of Don Juan.

Conversation Questions

Pair Work. Ask each other the following questions. If your partner asks for additional information, use your imagination to think of something. If you hear a very interesting response, share it with the class.

1. Did you learn to ride a bicycle **right off the bat?**
2. My friend wants a job in a bank, but she is not good with numbers. The bank president asked me if she would be good at the job. Should I **go to bat for** her?
3. In your country, do women have a lot, a little, or hardly any **clout** in politics?
4. What famous person would **be a hit** if he or she visited your country?
5. What kind of person are you likely to **hit it off** with?
6. On the international scene, what nation do you think really **plays hardball?**
7. Do you think I should **touch base with** my lawyer before signing my book contract?

8. The president is going to **kick off** a fund-raising campaign next week with a dinner at my house. And you are invited. Do you want to come?

9. If you were offered a job, starting tomorrow, at $40,000, would you **go for it?**

10. Have you **lost your touch** at anything (for example, cooking, making friends, playing pool)?

11. In your family, who **calls the shots?**

12. If I said that the United States was going to win the next World Cup in soccer, what two idioms could you use to respond?

13. If I lost $1,000 gambling, would you say, **"Those are the breaks,"** or would you be sympathetic? Why?

14. If you lost $100 at a casino, would you try to **break even,** or would you accept your miserable fate and go home?

15. Do you have a good shot at becoming famous, or is it **a long shot?**

Understanding and Speaking

Pair Work. Complete the conversation with the idioms in the list. Read your conversation with a partner, and then switch roles and read it again.

calling the shots	*lost your touch*	*kick off*
give me a break (used twice)	*hit it off*	*go for it*
a long shot	*those are the breaks*	*be a hit*

Carlos: I am supposed to meet a sorcerer who is 500 years old!

Flora: _____1_____! Even witches die.

Carlos: Not this one. I'm worried, though. What does this guy want from me—my soul?

Flora: Carlos, we are the sorcerer's apprentices. Once you start on this path, you can't turn back. You have to accept it. Terror is the price of knowledge.

_____2_____ of the game.

Carlos: This sorcerer is supposed to give me a gift, some power. But what if he wants my soul in return?

Flora: I guess you should _____3_____. It's too late to turn back. I'm surprised at you. You have always faced the challenges Don Juan set for you.

Carlos: I trusted Don Juan. But he's not _____4_____ here. It's some 500-year-old wizard who transforms himself into a young woman.

Flora: Maybe you'll get lucky and she'll be cute. You might _____
5
with her.

Carlos: _____. 500 years old!
6

Flora: But women adore you. You haven't _____, have you? Just
7
think, if you survive, you can write another book about it. It will

_____. And come September, you can _____
8   9
a new series of readings at colleges all over the country.

Carlos: Do you think I'll survive?

Flora: It's _____, but it's your fate to go. As they say in _Star_
10
Wars, "May the force be with you."

Creative Conversation

Complete the conversation, using the numbered hints. Read the conversation twice with
a partner, changing roles the second time. Do not look at your partner's text. You must
remember how your partner filled in the blanks so that you can respond in an appropriate way.

1. room or place, but not kitchen (garage)   4. other rooms
2. animal or insect (snake, roach)   5. amount of time (six months)
3. other rooms   6. amount of time

Sally: Harry, if you don't clean up the _____, I'm going to
1
get my witch friend Flora to turn you into a _____.
2

Harry: **Give me a break,** Sally. The _____ is not so bad.
1
Besides, why don't you get her to say "_Abracadabra,_* the

_____ is clean"? Then, like magic, it's clean.
1

Sally: The _____ is too hard for a witch to undertake. It
1
needs a real man.

Harry: Hey, Sal, in the kitchen you **call the shots.** The _____
1
is my domain. I'm the boss there.

Sally: OK. Here's the deal. You clean the _____; I clean the
1
_____ and the _____. So we
3   4
break even on cleaning.

* _Abracadabra: word associated with magic and with witches._

Harry: **Break even? Not by a long shot!** The _____
₁

hasn't been cleaned in _____. It will take
₅

_____ to clean it.
₆

Sally: OK, then let's switch. I'll do the _____, and you do
₁

the rest.

Harry: Boy, you really know how to **play hardball.** I hate to admit it, but I'd

rather turn into a _____ than clean house.
₂

Sentence Completion

Finish these sentences.

1. I learned to _____ **right off the bat.**

2. I'd **go to bat for** you if _____

_____.

3. If my _____ **had** more **clout,** _____

_____.

4. I think _____ is going to **be a hit** because _____

_____.

5. My friends _____ and _____ **hit it**

off because _____

_____.

6. If my company asks me to relocate to New York, I'll **play hardball.** I'll _____

_____.

7. Do you think we should **touch base** before _____

_____.

8. What do you think of this idea for **kicking off** the twenty-fifth anniversary

reunion of our high school class: _____

_____.

9. My best friend asked me if he/she should _____

_____, and I said, **"Go for it."**

10. I used to be able to pick out good wines for nine dollars a bottle, but lately I've **lost my touch.** Yesterday, for example, _____

_____.

11. Frankly, if I were **calling the shots** in the White House, the first thing I'd do is

_____.

12. You lost your house, your Nintendo, your stamp collection. **Those are the breaks** when _____.

13. We went to Paris for two weeks in April, and the first seven days it rained constantly. But then I guess we **broke even** on weather because _____

_____.

14. **Give me a break!** That horse you bet on _____

_____.

15. It would be **a long shot** for me to _____

_____.

16. You think _____ is a nice place to visit?! **Not by a long shot.** The truth is _____

_____.

Writing and Speaking

Write six Conversation Questions similar to the ones on pages 172–173, using idioms from this chapter. Then ask and answer these new questions with a partner.

1. _____

_____

2. _____

_____

3. _____

_____

4. _____

_____

5. _____

_____

6. _____

_____

American Art 101

Look at the painting *Between Rounds* (1899) by Thomas Eakins and use five idioms from this chapter to tell what is happening in the painting, or how you feel about the painting, or what one of the people in the painting might say.

Example: If the opponent knocks the boxer out with an illegal punch, the two men in his corner will go to bat for him and complain to the referee.

1. _____

_____

2. _____

_____

3. _____

_____

4. _____

_____

5. _____

_____

_____

Rewriting Using Idioms

Rewrite the following piece of art criticism, using idioms from this chapter and preserving the sense of the passage. You will have to do more than simply substitute phrases for the italicized words: sometimes you will have to change the structure of the sentence.

This painting stops time and movement for us. We see this especially in the part of the painting where the boxer pulls down the ropes. Notice the man in the boxer's corner, urging him, probably encouraging him to *accomplish it*. And notice the timekeeper at the bottom, waiting to hit the bell that will *start* the next round.

This painting was not an immediate *success*. Critics who had a lot of *influence* loved European Impressionism and did not see Eakins's genius *instantly*.

And just a bit of trivia that you won't find in any art book: the boxer, Billy Smith, was also known as Mysterious Billy Smith for his tendency to growl in an opponent's ear. And when the opponent turned to the referee to say, in effect, *"I don't believe this,"* Billy would hit him.

Presentation

Prepare a short presentation (up to five minutes) to the class on any topic you wish. Use as many of the idioms in this chapter as you feel comfortable with.

> Suggested Topics
>
> A popular singer in your country
>
> A person with a lot of clout in your country
>
> How to make a dish (for example, sushi, an apple tart, an omelet)
>
> Sorcery in your country

chapter 15

BASIC METAPHOR
• Life Is a Game

INTRODUCTION As the philosopher Ludwig Wittgenstein pointed out, the word *game* is nearly impossible to define. In the previous chapter, we dealt with games that are played with balls, but a ball is not necessary for a game. Chess is a game, and sports are games. In this chapter, we will consider idioms that come from a wide variety of sports.

WARM-UP Pick a sport (besides baseball, American football, and pool), and explain to a group of three or four how that sport is played. Learn as much of the vocabulary as necessary to explain the sport as best you can. Ask other group members for help with words you do not know.

When the probability of something happening is low, we say that the odds are against it. Do you think the odds are for or against two people in this class having the same birthday? Find out people's birthdays and test your guess.

SPORTS

1 have a shot at / take a shot at
Have an opportunity to succeed at / try to succeed at

Picture it!
Success is the target. If it is possible for you to shoot (a ball, an arrow, etc.) at it, you have the opportunity to succeed.

Example:
You'd better start training if you want to **have a shot at** finishing the Boston marathon. My friend Angela is going to **take a shot at it.**

2 be a tossup
Be an outcome that can be decided in two different ways, with equal probability

Picture it!
To start a basketball game, the referee tosses the ball up between two players whose teams in theory have an equal chance to gain possession of the ball. In a football game, the referee tosses up a coin to see who will kick the ball off. The probability of getting *heads* or *tails*—the names of the two sides of a coin—is equal.

Example:
No one knows who is going to win the election. It**'s a tossup.**

 3 **high stakes** (*noun*) / **high-stakes** (*adjective*)
Serious potential consequences

4 **the odds are**
The probability is

Picture it!
The stakes are the money that is bet or gambled. The money is said to be at stake, meaning that it is at risk of being won or lost. *High stakes* means "a lot of money."

Picture it!
When playing a game of chance, players try to calculate the probability (odds) that the card or number they want will come up.

Example:
Our construction company is trying to get the contract to build a new football stadium. We're playing for **high stakes.**

Example:
I think **the odds are** pretty good that you'll pass the course, especially since the teacher is your uncle.

 5 **a level playing field**
A fair environment

Picture it!
Level means "flat." If the field is inclined, then the team going downhill has an unfair advantage.

Example:
I want to start a telephone company, but I can't because it's not **a level playing field.** A major phone company owns all the telephone lines already in place.

 6 no sweat
There is no difficulty

Picture it!
If you exert yourself, trying hard, you will sweat (perspire). But if the activity is easily done, you will not sweat.

Example:
A: How was the chemistry test? Did you pass?
B: **No sweat.** I finished in ten minutes, and I'm sure I got an A.
(**Note:** *This idiom is usually used by itself, instead of in a sentence.*)

7 know the ropes
Know the details because of long experience

Picture it!
A boxer who has boxed a long time knows if the ropes in a given boxing ring are tight or loose, so he knows how they will react when he leans against them. The ring in the drawing above corresponds to any area of life.

Example:
Bill has worked here for forty years. He really **knows the ropes,** so if you ever need to get something done, ask him. He'll be able to help you.

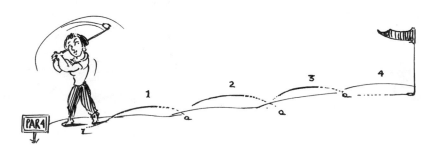

 8 be par for the course
Be what is expected, normal (often used negatively)

Picture it!
Par is the number of shots a good player is expected to take to hit a golf ball into the hole. A golf course has eighteen holes, and par for most courses is 72.

Example:
Joan got fired, but that's **par for the course.** They fire everyone who criticizes the company's environmental policy.

 9 beat someone to the punch
Do something before another person does it

Picture it!

Two boxers have the same intention: each one wants to punch the other first. If we both punch and you hit me first, you win. You beat me to the punch.

Example:

Lyle and I both wanted to go out with Tracy. I called her at nine o'clock, but Lyle had already called her at eight. He **beat me to the punch.**

 10 beats me
Puzzles me, I don't know

Picture it!

Beats means "defeats." If you fail to know something, you are defeated in your attempt to know it.

Examples:

A: Peter, what is the solution to this equation?
B: **Beats me,** Professor. I can't figure it out.

11 play ball
Cooperate

Picture it!

Our team can sit down and do nothing—in which case there is no game—or it can **play ball,** that is, join in the game.

Example:

My company offered my old boss a huge salary to come out of retirement, but she wouldn't **play ball.**

12 **throw in the towel**
Surrender, concede defeat

Picture it!
When a boxer's trainer throws a towel into the ring, he concedes that his fighter has lost. (Originally, the idiom was *throw in the sponge*. If you look at the Eakins painting in Chapter 14, you will see that there is a sponge in the bucket in the corner.)

Example:
The conservative party is way behind in the polls. They should just **throw in the towel.**

Understanding and Using Idioms

Complete the sentences with idioms from the list.

a level playing field	*high-stakes*	*take a shot at*
the odds are	*a tossup*	*beats me*
beaten me to the punch	*know the ropes*	*no sweat*
threw in the towel	*par for the course*	*play ball*

Professor Hawkins Lectures on Chaos Theory

Will it ever be possible to control the weather? _____1_____. Weather is chaotic. It is essentially unpredictable, except in the short run. Rain today, snow tomorrow—or maybe a tornado. It is _____2_____. Not knowing is _____3_____. Even if you have been a meteorologist—a weather expert—for thirty years and have a super computer, you can't tell what the weather will be like in New England a week from now. It doesn't matter how well you

_____4_____.

But predicting the weather is a _____5_____ game. We could save many lives if we could predict tornadoes in time to warn people.

_____ that we never will be able to predict the weather with
_____6

sufficient accuracy. Most scientists long ago _____ on that. They
_____7

cynically suggest that the only way we'll be able to predict the weather is if the

"weather gods" _____. If they do, we could even control the weather.
_____8

   In the meantime, perhaps there is hope in the fact that within the chaos of

weather there is order. It is a disorderly order, and this realization has produced a

revolution in science. Let me _____ explaining this via the Butterfly
_____9

Effect. The term comes from the notion that a butterfly stirring the air in Beijing

can influence the weather in New York a month later. Think of snowflakes: every

one is different, but there is an organizing principle. They are all basically the same

thing, even though no two are ever identical. Nature is not _____.
_____10

It is irregular, fragmentary, yet it has organizing principles. This is the essence

of chaos theory, a theory I would have discovered if a few other scientists had

not _____.
_____11

   Of course my husband insists that he can infallibly predict the weather. "Do

you want to know what the weather will be during the first week of July?

_____," he says. "Rain, guaranteed. It always rains during
_____12

our vacation."

Conversation Questions

Pair Work. Ask each other the following questions. If your partner asks for additional
information, use your imagination to think of something. If you hear a very interesting
response, share it with the class.

1. If you were offered the possibility of being the first ESL student to accompany
   a group of astronauts to the moon, would you **take a shot at** it? Why or why not?

2. If there were a presidential election in your country tomorrow, would the result
   be a tossup, or would one candidate be far ahead of the other?

3. Where in the world right now is there a **high-stakes** negotiation going on?

4. In the United States, we are brought up to believe that political success is **a
   level playing field,** that every kid **has a shot at** being president. Is this true in
   your country? Why or why not?

5. At a recent party I asked if anyone could fix my computer, and my ten-year-old
   nephew said, "Sure. **No sweat.**" Should I trust him?

6. In your country, is it **par for the course** for the same party to win most
   elections?

7. My brother wants to take a day off from work and go fishing, but I'm afraid his boss will find out and fire him. My brother says not to worry, that he **knows the ropes.** But he's only been working there for six months. Is that long enough to **know the ropes?**

8. I've been trying to win the Yale Series of Younger Poets contest for twenty years. Do you think it's time for me to **throw in the towel?**

9. Describe a situation where someone **beat you to the punch.**

10. I asked this woman with a Rolex watch, who was sitting next to me in the coffee shop of the Ritz-Carlton hotel, what time it was. And she said, **"Beats me."** Why do you think she said that?

11. Suppose the math teacher was very trusting and left the room during the final examination and one of the students suggested that all of you share answers. Would you **play ball?**

Understanding and Speaking

Pair Work. Albert Einstein and the artist Oskar Kokoschka are at a café in Vienna in 1921. Complete their conversation with the idioms in the list. Read the conversation with a partner, and then switch roles and read it again.

a tossup	*the odds*	*par for the course*
take a shot at	*no sweat*	*beats me*
beat me to the punch		

Albert: So, Oskar, would you like to do my portrait?

Oskar: I might _____ it.
                              1

Albert: How much would it cost?

Oskar: Everything is relative, Al.

Albert: Ha! But you know, Oskar, art is all about details. I have some Dutch ink drawings from 1600 with miniature cows and trees at the horizon. Details, Oskar. God is in the details.

Oskar: Exactly what I was going to say! You _____.
                                                              2
And the details. What to put in, what to leave out. It is
_____, sometimes. If I did a portrait of you,
          3
should I have electricity coming out of your hair? Or cows?

Albert: _____. You're the artist, not me. But I really love
                    4
your work, Oskar. So, what are _____ that I can get
                                                5
you to do it this afternoon for fifty dollars?

Oskar: This afternoon? That's _____ for you famous people.
6

Everything has to fit your schedule.

Albert: What do you want? I'm a busy person, relatively speaking. How about

tomorrow morning?

Oskar: Tomorrow morning? _____. As long as you're on
7

time. Not like your friend Heisenberg. I could never be certain when

he'd arrive.

Creative Conversation

Complete the conversation between Bart and his new physics teacher, Murray Gellman.
Use the numbered hints below. Read the conversation twice with a partner, changing
roles the second time. Do not look at your partner's text. You must remember how your
partner filled in the blanks so that you can respond in an appropriate way.

1. short adjective (smart)

2. place (the world, Moscow)

3. odds (2 to 1, 10 to 1, etc.)

4, 5. places to go on a date (McDonald's, the zoo)

Murray: Hi. I'm Murray Gellman and I'm the _____-est
1

person in _____.
2

Bart: Wow! That's really great. But there's this woman I saw on TV who

claimed to be the _____-est person in
1

_____. I guess she **beat you to the punch.**
2

Murray: That must be my ex-wife. She'll say anything to get on TV. That's **par for**

the course for her.

Bart: Do you think I **have a shot at** becoming the _____-
1

est person in the world some day?

Murray: As long as I'm living, I'd say **the odds are** _____
3

against it, but you could always **take a shot at it.**

Bart: Were you always _____? I mean, even when you
1

were a kid?

Murray: Yes. So you see it's not **a level playing field.** Some folks start out

_____-er than others.
1

Bart: So, tell me—I mean if you don't mind my asking—where did you take

the _____ -est woman in
                    1

_____ , when you went out on a date?
              2

Murray: I'd usually take her to either _____ or
                                                        4

_____ . It **was a tossup.**
              5

Sentence Completion

Finish these sentences.

1. _____ doesn't **have a shot at** _____

   _____ .

2. When _____ play against _____ for

   the championship, it will probably **be a tossup** because _____

   _____ .

3. My friends and I play cards every Friday night. But it's not a **high-stakes**

   game. I mean, _____

   _____ .

4. **The odds are** very good that I will _____ because _____

   _____ .

5. I have no chance to be _____ because it is not **a level**

   playing field. I mean, _____

   _____ .

6. Of course I can _____ . **No sweat.** And this should

   convince you: last year, I _____

   _____ .

7. It is **par for the course** for little boys to _____ and for

   little girls to _____

   _____ .

8. _____ **knows the ropes** of the music business in my

   country because _____

   _____ .

9. I want to _____,

   and I will. I'll never **throw in the towel.**

10. I wanted to _____,

    but _____ **beat me to the punch.**

11. Who is going to be president in 2012? **Beats me.** But I can tell you who it won't

    be: _____, because _____

    _____.

12. It would be good to have an international treaty or agreement to _____

    _____, but if one or more nations don't **play ball,**

    _____.

Writing and Speaking

Write six Conversation Questions similar to the ones on pages 184–185, using idioms from this chapter. Then ask and answer these new questions with a partner.

1. _____

   _____

2. _____

   _____

3. _____

   _____

4. _____

   _____

5. _____

   _____

6. _____

   _____

Presentation

Prepare a short presentation (up to five minutes) to the class on any topic you wish. Use as many of the idioms in this chapter as you feel comfortable with.

Suggested Topics

A career you would like to pursue

The worst career (or job) you can imagine

Racial discrimination

The weather, or climate, in

_____

answer key

Chapter 1
Understanding and Using Idioms

1. nuts, 2. eat it up, 3. opened a can of worms, 4. tossed out the idea, 5. to put my spin on, 6. on a back burner, 7. kick around, 8. leaves a bad taste in our mouths, 9. baloney, 10. food for thought, 11. fishy, 12. bounce another idea off you, 13. catch, 14. field questions, 15. ballpark figure, 16. on the ball, 17. swallow this hook, line, and sinker, 18. spill the beans

Chapter 2
Understanding and Using Idioms

1. points, 2. cutting-edge, 3. drive a hard bargain, 4. sharp, 5. take this into account, 6. hit the nail on the head, 7. tradeoff, 8. buy, 9. scratched the surface, 10. influence peddling

Chapter 3
Understanding and Using Idioms

1. shed some light, 2. as far as I know, 3. beyond the shadow of a doubt, 4. in the dark, 5. come straight to the point, 6. along the same lines, 7. blanket statements, 8. in a whole new light, 9. dawned on you, 10. see the light, 11. jump to the conclusion, 12. on the right track, 13. get across, 14. beat around the bush, 15. as plain as day, 16. covered a lot of ground

Understanding and Speaking

1. in a whole new light, 2. it dawned on me, 3. in the dark, 4. jump to the conclusion, 5. beyond the shadow of a doubt, 6. along the same lines, 7. see the light

Chapter 4
Understanding and Using Idioms

1. don't hold water, 2. let me put it this way, 3. jump in, 4. get sidetracked, 5. get a word in edgewise, 6. shot down, 7. on shaky ground, 8. stuck to my guns, 9. take flak for, 10. duck the issue, 11. switch gears, 12. jump on the bandwagon

Chapter 5
Understanding and Using Idioms

1. blow you away, 2. dying to, 3. cracked, 4. crack you up, 5. weathered the storm, 6. knockout, 7. having short fuses, 8. blew up, 9. come apart at the seams, 10. crackpot, 11. to die for, 12. kills me, 13. bowled, 14. scared to death, 15. floored, 16. pull yourselves together, 17. blow off some steam, 18. falls apart, 19. blow over

Understanding and Speaking

1. scared me to death, 2. dying to, 3. blew me away, 4. blowing off some steam, 5. crack me up, 6. blew up, 7. pulls himself together, 8. crackpot, 9. kill

Chapter 6
Understanding and Using Idioms

1. dough, 2. were peanuts, 3. make a killing, 4. slash prices, 5. in the red, 6. cut-throat, 7. reap, 8. mean business, 9. make a killing, 10. skimming the profits, 11. pay through the nose

Understanding and Speaking

1. peanuts, 2. cut-throat, 3. in the red, 4. slashed, 5. peanuts, 6. making a killing, 7. dough, 8. skim

Chapter 7

Understanding and Using Idioms

1. filthy rich, 2. hit intellectual pay dirt, 3. wiped out, 4. go down the drain, 5. foot the bill, 6. have deep pockets, 7. clean up, 8. taken to the cleaners, 9. cleaned out, 10. moneygrubbing, 11. the bottom line, 12. money launderers

Chapter 8

Understanding and Using Idioms

1. pin me down, 2. string men along, 3. tied to his mother's apron strings, 4. hit me up for, 5. a soft touch, 6. rein in, 7. up in the air, 8. cut me some slack, 9. gotten out of hand, 10. carried away, 11. get ahold of, 12. get a grip, 13. fly off the handle, 14. at the end of their rope, 15. pulling strings, 16. out of my hands

Understanding and Speaking

1. up in the air, 2. flew off the handle, 3. stringing her along, 4. get ahold of yourself, 5. get out of hand, 6. rein in, 7. hit you up for, 8. a soft touch

Chapter 9

Understanding and Using Idioms

1. black sheep, 2. chickened out, 3. turkeys, 4. chewing out, 5. bearish, 6. bullish, 7. the cream of the crop, 8. monkey business, 9. bitched, 10. clammed up, 11. wolfed down, 12. big cheese, 13. weasel out of, 14. monkey with, 15. ahead of the pack, 16. couch potatoes

Chapter 10

Understanding and Using Idioms

1. missed the boat, 2. get off the ground, 3. get your feet wet, 4. starting out on the wrong foot, 5. going downhill, 6. paves the way, 7. end of the road, 8. all downhill from here, 9. giving you the green light, 10. on the verge of, 11. passed away

Chapter 11

Understanding and Using Idioms

1. rocked the boat, 2. burn their bridges, 3. in the same boat, 4. get cold feet, 5. take it in stride, 6. up and running, 7. follow in their footsteps, 8. gone through, 9. in the wake of, 10. on the fast track, 11. social climber, 12. drag your feet, 13. on board

Understanding and Speaking

1. follow in the footsteps, 2. on the fast track, 3. on board, 4. social climber, 5. took it in stride, 6. in the same boat, 7. rock the boat, 8. in the wake of

Chapter 12

Understanding and Using Idioms

1. hit twenty, 2. in a rut, 3. ran into problems, 4. a lot riding on, 5. came through for, 6. between a rock and a hard place, 7. clear sailing, 8. jumped the gun, 9. went through with, 10. fall behind, 11. in a tight spot, 12. start from scratch, 13. run for, 14. cooped up

Chapter 13

Understanding and Using Idioms

1. wheeler-dealers, **2.** the deck stacked against you, **3.** bum deal, **4.** ace, **5.** holding all the cards, **6.** play your cards right, **7.** the luck of the draw, **8.** bluffing, **9.** call our bluff, **10.** lay my cards on the table, **11.** fold, **12.** making a deal, **13.** up my sleeve, **14.** deal with

Chapter 14

Understanding and Using Idioms

1. kick off, **2.** hit it off, **3.** right off the bat, **4.** not by a long shot, **5.** go for it, **6.** be a hit, **7.** played hardball, **8.** clout, **9.** go to bat for me, **10.** a long shot, **11.** those are the breaks, **12.** losing your touch, **13.** give me a break, **14.** called the shots, **15.** break even, **16.** touch base

Understanding and Speaking

1. give me a break, **2.** those are the breaks, **3.** go for it, **4.** calling the shots, **5.** hit it off, **6.** give me a break, **7.** lost your touch, **8.** be a hit, **9.** kick off, **10.** a long shot

Chapter 15

Understanding and Using Idioms

1. beats me, **2.** a tossup, **3.** par for the course, **4.** know the ropes, **5.** high-stakes, **6.** the odds are, **7.** threw in the towel, **8.** play ball, **9.** take a shot at, **10.** a level playing field, **11.** beaten me to the punch, **12.** no sweat

Understanding and Speaking

1. take a shot at, **2.** beat me to the punch, **3.** a tossup, **4.** beats me, **5.** the odds, **6.** par for the course, **7.** no sweat

photo credits